Consumer Market and Consumer Behaviour

A Case Study

Consumer Market and Consumer Behaviour

A Case Study

H. Ramananda Singh

AKANSHA PUBLISHING HOUSE
NEW DELHI • GUWAHATI • VISAKHAPATNAM

AKANSHA PUBLISHING HOUSE
4649-B/21, Ansari Road
Darya Ganj, New Delhi - 110 002
Ph.: 23263193 / 9811582579 / 09435116718
Fax: 011-23263193
Email: ektabooks@yahoo.com
www.akanshapublishinghouse.com

Consumer Market and Consumer Behaviour: A Case Study

First Published 2010

ISBN 978-81-8370-224-9

PRINTED IN INDIA

Published by Akansha Publishing House, New Delhi and Printed at S.N. Printers, Delhi.

Dedicated

to

My parents

Contents

Preface

With the unfolding of the 21st century, the business environment that the marketers find today is entirely different from what they used to experience 10 years ago. What one finds today is the global environment and global market in which time and space is reduced enormously with the evolution of a new communication system through computer networking.

India, in order to keep pace with the changes taking place worldwide, liberalised her economy with the announcement of a new industrial policy in July 1991. Along with the changes in the economic and communication environment, consumer markets of durable and non-durable goods have also changed.

N.N. Sachitanand (1999) reasons that as a result of economic liberalisation that lifted the qualitative and the quantitative restrictions under the new trade policies and the country coming under the ambit of WTO, the fast moving consumer goods market in India has undergone radical changes. Some of the major drivers in the Indian fast moving consumer goods market have been:

- Progressive reduction in excise duties in major fast moving consumer goods product category.
- Considerable easing of licensing restriction

- Rapid extension of media reach, especially TV.
- Almost double rate of economic growth as compared to the past and this growth spans, all levels of society.

For the consumer, the change has been heralded by a very large number of foreign brands now available legally on shop shelves which were earlier procured through the grey market. The durable goods after having negative growth rate in the mid nineties the market grows at about 20 percent per annum. Indian consumer never has had a wide variety to choose from, not only in brands but also in technologies, ranging from semi-automatic, mechanical contraption to highly automated "intelligent" appliance.

The competition is fierce and the consumer has benefited not just by price slashes but deferred payment, home deliveries, gifts and extended free service. In the changing market scenario of consumer durable and non- durable goods, new products are launched at an astonishing pace and are available everywhere in shorter time. Marketers increase their use of branding, product differentiation, advertising and promotion. While these changes are taking place, consumers do not live in isolation and their needs and wants are also not static. Consumer's taste, preference, lifestyle, etc. are also continuously changing with the changing of socio-economic and cultural environments. Consumers of today are well informed and have become more selective in their choice of goods. Thus the marketers find it harder to predict buyers' response.

In today's complex situation of fierce competition in the market, marketer could not sell what he offers to sell or produces. Marketer can successfully sell only what is desired by the consumers. In such situations, for accomplishing the objectives of the business organizations, marketers need to monitor continuously the changes that are taking place in the consumer market and consumer behaviour before formulating marketing strategies for the target market.

On the basis of information about the consumer market and consumer behaviour, a marketer has to take decisions about the product, price, place and promotion that best suit the consumer segment(s).

In the present business scenario, there will be winners and losers. Losers are those who do not bring anything unique to the consumers and winners are those who carefully analyse the need, identify opportunities, and create value- laden offer for target consumer groups that the competitors cannot match.

Consumer durable and non-durable market of Manipur is a small segment of the Indian domestic market. As per the census 2001, the population of Manipur is 23, 88,634 persons which is 0.23% of the population of all India.

In Manipur there are not many industries worth mentioning which cater the need of consumer durable and non-durable goods for the households of Manipur. Almost all the non-durable goods such as toilet soap, shampoo, tooth paste, etc. and durable goods such as TV, Refrigerator, washing machine, etc. use by the people of Manipur come from outside the state. So, Manipur a small segment of India's domestic market with its decadal growth rate of population of 30.02% merits to draw attention of the marketers while formulating their marketing strategies for Manipur market. So far, studies were not conducted regarding the consumer market and consumer behaviour of Manipur from the marketing management perspective. Study of consumer market and consumer behaviour will benefit the consumers of Manipur, marketers, upcoming entrepreneurs and the policy makers of Manipur.

This book is substantially based on the findings of the Doctoral research in Management carried out at Manipur University.

In this book the author has made an attempt to integrate the consumer market and consumer behaviour and the marketing strategies with special reference to nondurable goods (toilet soap) and durable goods (TV).

Information provided by this book can assist marketers in recognizing and reacting to marketing opportunities and problems in Manipur. Knowledge of consumer markets and consumer behaviour of TV and toilet soap will enable to draw an inference of the other similar products also.

H. Ramananda Singh

Acknowledgements

In the completion and production of this book many people have been enormously helpful. It is a pleasure to acknowledge their contributions and I am deeply grateful to all of them.

Language has no words to express my gratitude to Prof. V.P.Giri, retired Director of Manipur Institute of Management Studies. I am highly indebted to him for his invaluable insights, suggestions and continued moral support throughout the research work. He has been a constant source of inspiration in the completion of this book.

I am especially grateful to Prof. U. R. Dhar, Gauhati University for his invaluable suggestions and encouragement.

Dr. S.K. Sharma, Prof. & Head, Department of Management Science, Technical Institute of Textile and Sciences, Haryana, has been a source of moral support and encouragement right from the beginning, I am grateful to him. I also wish to express my sincere thanks to three Professors; Prof. S.S. Khanka, Tejpur University, Prof. A.R. Rehman, Dibrugarh University and Prof. Apurbananda Mazumdar, Assam University who have been sources of my inspiration in completing this work. I would particularly like to thank to the faculty members of MIMS, Dr (Mrs) Memcha L., Dr. Ch. Ibohal Meitei, Dr. L. Jobonkumar Sharma, Shri Ksh. Kunjabi Singh, and Shri Lai Prabhakar for their continuous suggestions and highly constructive comments.

I would like to thank Shri Ksh. Jugeshor Singh, Deputy Director of Sports, Manipur University and Shri S. Rajen Singh, A.E. Manipur University for giving morale support and helping me considerably.

I owe my heartfelt gratitude to Dr. Gurdas Das, HOD, Humanities Deptt. of NIT, Silchar for giving me the support and giving me the opportunity to complete this book.

Thanks are due to my friends Shri Kh. Premananda Singh, Shri S Somorendro Singh and Shri Chayan Paul who have been constant sources of encouragement.

I am indebted to my parents, Shri H. Komol Singh and Shrimati H. Ibeton Devi for their blessings.

It is my privilege to thank my sister Shrimati H. Merina Devi and my brothers H. Premananda Singh and H. Bobby Singh for their endearing support.

Last but not the least, I express my gratitude to my wife Shrimati L. Indira Devi for her continuous support and sharing the hardship throughout the work.

H. Ramananda Singh

1

Introduction

Introduction

Every business organisation comes into existence with the aim of accomplishing two main objectives, namely economic objective and social objective. These two objectives can be accomplished only if the product produced by the organisation satisfies the needs and wants of the consumers. In today's competitive marketing scenario, the marketer cannot sell the product what he offers to sell or produces but he can successfully sell only what is desired by the consumer. But what the consumer desire is not easy to comprehend. This poses a big problem before the marketer. This problem can be solved only by getting the necessary information regarding the consumers and market conditions.

If the information reveals that consumers are not satisfied with the marketer's products or services, he makes decision to adapt it accordingly. This helps the marketers to raise the level of performance of the organization. Marketer after understanding the needs and wants of the consumers that make up the market takes decisions about the product, price, place and promotion that best suit the consumer segment(s) which is/are targeted (Fig 1).

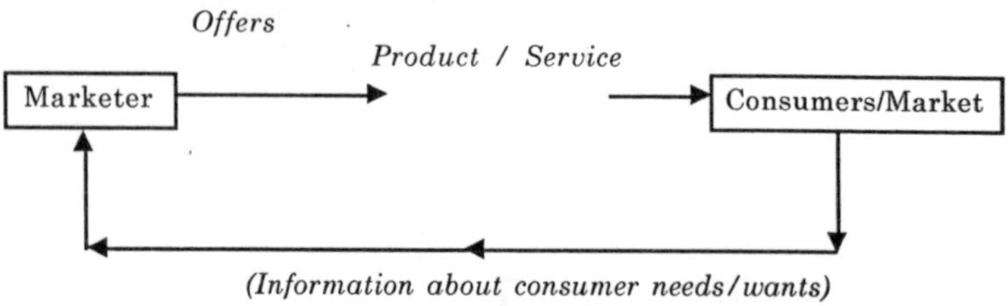

Fig. 1: Relationship between offers of marketers and needs and wants of Market

But the consumers do not live in isolation and their needs and wants are not static. They live within a macro and micro environments. These are the factors external to the consumers which indirectly influence them. The micro environments which include culture, subculture, social class, social group, personal and family influences are more influential than the macro environment. The larger socio-economic conditions of a country i.e. macro environments where the marketers find themselves to day are changing very fast. The changing socio-economic scenario together with micro-environment interacts with individual consumer's psychological factors which include motivation, perception, learning, personality and self concept and belief and attitude.

As a result of this interaction taste, preference, life style etc. of the consumer is also changing. Since the survival and growth of a company depends upon the satisfaction of the needs and wants of the consumers it serves, it is imperative for a marketer to monitor continuously the trend of the consumer market and its behaviour before a sound marketing plan can be developed or modified to serve the consumers.

"Management is the youngest of sciences and the oldest of arts and the consumer behaviour in management is a very young discipline. Various scholars and academician concentrated on it at a much later stage. It was during the 1950s that marketing concept developed, and thus the need to study the behaviour of consumers was recognized. Marketing starts with the needs of the customer and ends with his satisfaction. When everything revolves round the customer, then the study of the consumer behaviour becomes a necessity".[1]

Consumer refers to the individual consumer who purchases goods for his or her own personal use or for household use. Market is a set of all actual buyers of a product or services. And consumer market consists of individuals and households that buy goods and services for personal consumption.

Consumers of a product differ in region, age, sex, family size, family life cycle, income, occupation, education, social class, personality, lifestyle, occasion of purchase, usage rate, loyalty status, and attitude towards the product. Accordingly consumers market which is a set of all the consumers can be divided into various segments. Each of the segments has similarity in response to the stimuli or market offers of a business organization. According to Philip Kotler and Gary Armstrong, "consumer behaviour refers to the buying behaviour of final consumers - individuals and households who buy goods and services for personal consumption. All of these final consumers combined make up the consumer market."[2] Different consumers have various needs and they belong to various age, income, sex, educational and occupational groups. These consumers also purchase variety of goods and services. How the diverse consumers make their choice among the various products is an interesting issue. In a particular consumer market, consumer's behaviour is the product of the interaction between the individual's psychological influences and the environmental influences. Consumer's decision to purchase goods and services is generally influenced by how those are socially viewed.

"Behaviour is, therefore, determined by the individual's psychological makeup and the influence of the others. The dual influence has been summarized in the following simplified equation of behaviour.

$$B = f(P, E)$$

Consumer behaviour (B) is, therefore, the result of the interaction of the consumer's personal influences (P) and the pressures exerted upon them by outside forces in the environment (E). Understanding consumer behaviour requires that we understand the nature of these influences."[3]

Some of the important individual's psychological determinants that effect consumer behaviour are motivation, perception, learning, attitude, and personality and self-concept. And some of the external factors that affect the consumer behaviour are general socioeconomic condition, cultural influence, sub- cultural influence, social class influence and personal influence. These external factors can be bifurcated into macro and micro environment.

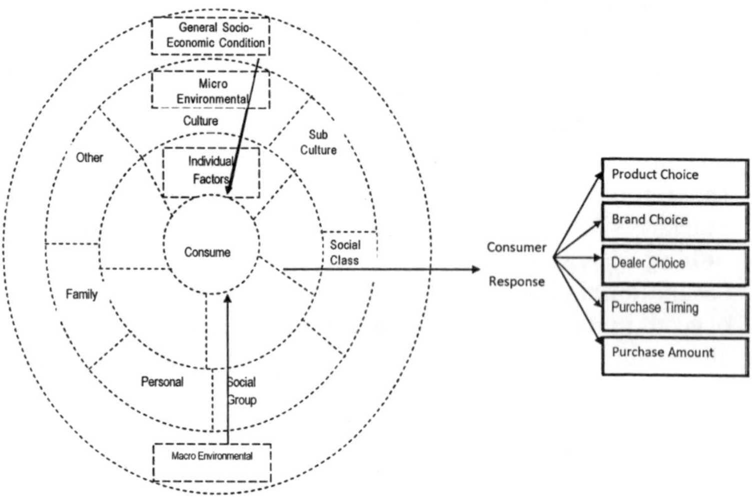

Broken lines (....) denote the force of inter and intra play amongst these factors. External environments (both Micro & Macro environments) do not directly affect the consumer but filter through individual determinants to influence the decision of the consumer. It is denoted by arrow (→).

Figure 2: Factors influencing consumer behaviour.

Moreover, consumers are bombarded by the marketing stimuli of various companies across the macro and micro environment that surround them. How the consumer responds to the stimuli in terms of product choice, brand choice, dealer choice, purchase timing and purchase amount is the product of the interaction of these stimuli with the macro and micro environmental factors and the individual's psychological factors.

Therefore, understanding of the consumer market and consumer behaviour is the most crucial factor in determining the success of the marketers. In earlier times, marketers could understand consumer through the daily experience of selling to them. But the growth in the size of firms and markets has turned the direct contact into almost unrealizable proposition in many cases. "Increasingly managers have had to turn to consumer research for answers to the most important questions about any market called the seven O's of the market place, such as:

Occupants	Who constitute the market?
Objects	What does the market buy?
Objective	Why does the market buy?
Organisation	Who participates in the buying?
Operations	How does the market buy?
Occasions	When does the market buy?
Outlets	Where does the market buy from?"[4]

On one side the consumers that make up the entire market possess different behaviour and on the other companies widely vary in their ability to serve different segments of the market. Rather than trying to compete in an entire market, sometimes against superior competitors, each company must identify the part of the market that it can best serve. Company should take the right decisions in respect of product, price, place, and promotion.

Decisions regarding the product include product variety, quality design, features, brand name, packaging, sizes, service, warranties and returns decisions.

Price decisions include the decisions on list price, discount, allowances, payment period and credit terms.

Place decisions include decision on channels, coverage, assortments, locations, inventory and transport.

And Promotion decisions include decisions on sales promotion, advertising, sales force, public relations and direct marketing.

Any wrong decision will cause loss to the company in terms of lose of consumers, good will and market share.

Keeping in view of the importance of consumer market and its behaviour for the success or otherwise of marketer, the topic "Consumer market and consumer buying behaviour: A case study of Manipur with special reference to consumer durable goods (TV) and consumer non durable goods (Toilet soap)" has been chosen for the study.

"Durable goods are tangible goods that normally survive many uses". Examples include TV, refrigerator, washing machine etc. whereas the "non-durable goods are the tangible goods that normally are consumed in one or few uses"v such as soap, tooth paste, shampoo etc. Consumer non-durable goods are consumed fast and purchased frequently.

Manipur has a total population of 23, 88,634 persons (Census 2001) and an estimated total of number of households 3, 99437 (approximately) comprising different community with different socio-economic and cultural backgrounds. Manipur depends largely on products manufactured outside the state for household consumption.

Though the population of Manipur is 0.23% of the total of all India, it deserves the attention of the marketers. For Manipur with its decadal growth rate of 30.02% which is higher than 21.34% of all India is a growing market segment of Indian domestic market.

If the detail information of consumer market and consumer behaviour of Manipur is available, it will be an immense help not only to the companies marketing their products in Manipur but also to the aspiring entrepreneurs of Manipur for formulating appropriate marketing strategies for Manipur market. Information obtained from this study may also render service to the policy makers of the state for its economic planning.

Need for the Study

The field of consumer market and consumer buying behaviour holds great interest to all the segments of people i.e. consumers, marketers, entrepreneurs and policy makers for industrial development of the country. Consumers benefit from insight into their consumption related decisions; what they buy, when they buy, why they buy, how they buy and the promotional influences that persuade them to buy. The study of consumer market and consumer buying behaviour will enable them to become better and wiser. To the marketers and future marketers, it is important to recognise why and how individuals make their consumption decisions. If marketers understand consumer market and consumer buying behaviours, they are able to predict their marketing strategies accordingly. Without doubt, marketers who understand consumer market and consumer behaviour have great competitive advantage in the market place. To the entrepreneur who plays an important role in developing and contributing to the economy of a nation, the information about consumer market and consumer behaviour will provide them ample opportunities for entrepreneurial venture.

To the policy makers, study of consumer market and consumer behaviour will provide the information needed for economic planning and optimum utilization of resources for the development of the nation. Information will enable them to identify the industries which require to be nurtured.

Objectives of Study

The main objective of the study is to examine the consumer market and consumer buying behaviour in Manipur with a view to assess its relevance and to suggest appropriate marketing strategies.

The specific objectives are:

i) To understand the consumer market of Manipur with special reference to non durable goods (toilet soap) in terms of parameters such as - brand availability, number of households using single or more brands, usage rate, monthly average consumption and expenditure, market share of brands, per capita consumption and the share of Manipur consumer market in the Indian domestic consumer market of toilet soap.

ii) To explore consumer market of Manipur with special reference to durable goods (TV) in the following aspects - number of households presently owning TV set(s), Number of households owning a single TV set or more TV sets, brand preferred by the people who do not presently owned TV set, shares of TV brands of the penetrated market, annual growth rate of TV sets purchase, brand presently available in Manipur, sales of TV sets in the year 2001, market share of TV brands and share of Manipur TV market in the Indian domestic market of TV.

iii) To examine consumer buying behaviour of non-durable goods (toilet soap) and durable goods (TV) in some important aspects such as - consumer's background, awareness level of different brands, sources of information, product factors, marketing factors, buying roles, consumer's preferable (use) brand, outlets of purchase, purchase amount, purchase occasions, mode of purchase, consumer's satisfaction with the brand presently in use, brand loyalty, types of buying behaviour and comparative study of consumer buying behaviour between non durable goods (toilet soap) and durable goods (TV).

iv) To assess the consumer buying decisions in relation to promotional strategies and reference groups.

v) To suggest appropriate marketing strategies for consumer non- durable goods (toilet soap) and durable goods (TV) markets of Manipur.

Hypothesis

The hypothesis governing the study is "The consumer of Manipur are falling prey to the strategies of the various marketing organisations as their buying decisions are far from sound and rational". Hence, the assumption that will govern the proposed study are (i) Consumer's brand preference is dependent on promotional strategies i.e. advertising, discount and free gift offers of the company. (ii) Consumer's brand preference is dependent on its reference group i.e. recommendation of friends, family, relatives and colleagues.

Research Methodology

The research methodology which has been adopted for conducting this study is discussed as under:

(a) Research design

The research design that is chosen is both exploratory

and conclusive in nature. Exploratory research is adopted for understanding the insights of the consumer market and consumer buying behaviour and Conclusive research for testing the formulated hypothesis.

(b) Data collection Method

i) For primary data, questionnaire method which is the cost suitable means for market survey has been adopted for procuring the primary data to take up the present work. As Good Scates says "The questionnaire method is useful instrument for collecting information. It can also be mentioned what the Pearson says "unity of all sciences consists of its method and not the materials alone". Regarding collection of data which is the major source of material, Mark Abram says, "A social survey is a process by which questionnaire, facts are collected about social aspects of a community's composition and activities". For the purpose of the study, structural undisguised questionnaire consisting of both open-ended and multiple choice questions is designed.

ii) For secondary data, National demographics, books, journals and census data of 2001 have been referred for inferring the present consumer market and consumer buying behaviour of toilet soap and TV.

(c) Sampling design

In all 752 households are taken from 4 valley districts and one hill district of Manipur out of the total of 9 districts. Method of selecting households to be chosen for the study is Area sampling. District-wise names of the area from where sample households are chosen along with the number of households covered from the area are given below.

District	*Name of the area*	*Number of households*
I. Bishnupur	Bishnupur	50
	Moirang	50
	Ningthoukhong	33
	Nambol	40
Bishnupur	Total	173
	Thoubal	50
II. Thoubal	Kakching	51
	Mayang Imphal	50
Thoubal	Total	151
	Khurai	40
	Khetrigao	40
III. Imphal East	Singjamei	40
	Langthabal	31
Imphal East	Total	151
	Uripok	50
	Tera	50
IV. Imphal West	Khumbong	40
	Thangal Bazar	39
Imphal West	Total	179
	Churchandpur	50
V. Churchandpur	Tuibong	48
Churchandpur	Total	98
Total number of households for the study		752

(d) Operational area of study

The study is conducted in 4 valley districts of Manipur (i.e. Thoubal District, Bishnupur District, Imphal East district and Imphal West District) and one hill district of Manipur (i.e. Churchandpur).

(e) Processing of data, findings and conclusion

Responses, which are obtained through questionnaire method, are presented in different tables showing the percentage of respondents or responses with respect to each item. Findings and conclusions are drawn on the basis of the data collected with proper interpretations relevant to the purpose of the study.

(f) Statistical tools for data analysis

The estimation of purchase and consumption value of toilet soap and TV sets in the Indian domestic market are done with the help of Time Series Analysis using least square methodw . For testing the assumption, which governs the hypothesis of the study, Kolmogrov Smirnov D Test x is used.

(g) Presentation format

Tabular and descriptive style of presentation is used. Tabular style of presentation is used for easy grasping of the whole data. Descriptive style of presentation is used with simple and clear language for clear understanding of information extracted from the figures given in the tables.

(h) Limitation of study

Out of the 9 district of Manipur, only 5 districts i.e., 4 (four) valley and one hill districts are covered for the study. Because of the law and order problem, 4 hill districts of Manipur could not be covered. Data for year wise purchase of toilet soap and TV set in the Indian domestic market are available up to 1993-94 and data for year wise consumption value of toilet soap and TV in the Indian domestic market are available up to 1997-98 only. So, data for the year 2001 are estimated on the basis of the past trend and used in the analysis of the present study.

Hence, conclusion drawn on its basis cannot be used as panacea. However certain useful generalization can definitely be made to the advantage of marketer, entrepreneur, and policy makers.

Study design

The entire report of the study has been presented in the following form.

Chapter One, "Introduction" attempts to introduce in brief the concept of consumer market and consumer behaviour highlighting its importance to the Business organization. Need for the study, Research methodology used and the design of the study are the other components of this chapter.

Chapter Two, "Conceptual Vision of Consumer Market and Consumer Buying Behaviour and its Implications to Business Organizations" covers the theoretical vision of consumer market and consumer behaviour, current trend of consumer behaviour and consumer oriented marketing strategy.

Chapter Three, "Present Scenario of Consumer Markets of Manipur" presents a comprehensive examination of consumer non-durable goods (toilet soap) and consumer durable goods (TV) markets of Manipur.

Chapter Four, "Present Scenario of Consumer Buying Behaviour in Manipur" explores the consumer buying behaviour of non-durable goods (toilet soap) and durable goods (TV) in Manipur.

While Chapter Five, "Consumer Buying Decisions vis-a-vis Promotional Strategies and Reference Groups" examines mathematically the importance of promotional strategies and reference groups in the consumer buying decisions. It begins with the testing of assumptions governing the hypothesis of the study and concludes with the validation of the hypothesis.

The last chapter entitled "Marketing Strategy Development for Non Durable Goods (Toilet Soap) and

Dubable Goods (TV) Markets of Manipur" presents the conclusions and discusses the appropriate marketing strategies for Manipur consumer market.

NOTES

1. Khan Martin, *Consumer Behaviour,* New Age International Publisher, 2001 edition, p. 2.
2. Kotler, Philip and Armstrong, Gary; *Principles of Marketing,* Prentice Hall of India, Eastern Economy Edition, 9th edition p. 171.
3. Rathor, B.S, *Advertising Management,* Himalaya Publishing House, First Edition, reprint 1990, p. 71.
4. Kotler, Philip; *Marketing Management,* Prentice Hall of India, 7th Edition, 1991, p. 163.
5. *Ibid.,*
6. *Ibid.,*
7. Gupta, S.P.; *Statistical Method,* Revised Edition, 1995, Sultan Chand and Sons Publishers, New Delhi, p. E-14.25.
8. Donald S. Tull and Del I. Hawkins, *Marketing Research - Measurement and Methods,* 6th edition, Prentice Hall of India, New Delhi, 1996, pp. 645-646.

2

Conceptual Vision of Consumer Market and Consumer Buying Behaviour and its Implications to Business Organizations

Introduction

Business organisations endeavour to serve buyers/end users of the product better than their competitors. It is because of the patronage of the end users that the organisation survives and grows. And the end users of the product which are generally referred to as consumer is regarded as the kings in today's competitive market. The success or failure of the business organisation depends upon how well it serves the consumers. Thus analysing business market and its behaviour and chalking out appropriate marketing strategies that satisfy the needs and wants of the consumers is primary concern of the business organisation. This chapter explores the theoretical aspects of consumer market and consumer behaviour and its implication to business organisation.

Important aspects covered in this chapter are:

i) Consumer market

ii) Market segmentation

iii) Consumer behaviour

iv) Buying roles

v) Types of buying behaviour

vi) Consumer's decision-making process

vii) Four views of consumer decision-making

viii) Approaches to studying consumer behaviour

ix) Current trend in consumer behaviour

x) Consumer oriented view of marketing strategy.

Consumer Market

Consumer market is a combination of two terms—'consumer' and 'market'.

Consumer

"The term Consumer is often used to describe two different kinds of consuming entities; the personal consumer and the organizational consumer".[1]

The term personal consumer is used to refer to the consumer who buys goods and services for own personal consumption. For example, tooth paste, toilet soap, etc. are purchased for personal consumption and TV, washing machine, etc. are purchased for household uses. In each of the cases products are bought for final use by individuals who are referred to as end users or ultimate consumers.

The other type of consumers i.e. organisational consumers—purchase products in order to run their organization. Manufacturing companies must buy the raw material and other components needed to manufacture and sell their own products/services. Despite the importance of both the types of consumers i.e. personal and organisational, this research is focused on individual consumer who purchases for personal use or for his household use.

Market

The term market has acquired many meaning over the years. Traditionally, a market was a physical place where buyers and sellers gathered to exchange goods and services.

Medieval town had market squares where sellers brought their goods and buyers shopped for goods. According to Sidgwick,[2] a market is a body of persons in such commercial relations that each can easily acquaint himself with the rates at which certain kinds of exchanges of goods or services are, from time to time, made by the other.

In the words of Jevons[3] the word Market has been generalized so as to mean any body or persons who are in intimate business and carry on extensive transactions in any commodity.

According to Benham[4], Market is any area over which buyers and sellers are in closed touch with one another, either directly or through dealers that the price attainable in one part of the market affects the prices paid in the other market.

To an economist, a market describes all the buyers and sellers who transact over some goods or services.

To a marketer "A market is a set of actual and potential buyers of a product."[5] A market is a set of buyers. Despite the different meanings attached to the term market, for the purpose of the study it refers to the set of actual and potential buyers of a product. By combining the two terms consumer and market, consumer market can be defined as the set of all actual and potential buyers who purchase products/services for personal consumption or for household uses.

Market Segmentation

Consumers of a market are many and they are widely scattered. They belong to different age groups, income groups, educational level groups and a have different needs / wants and buying pattern. But "a market segment consists of a large identifiable group within a market with similar wants, purchasing powers, geographical location, buying attitude or buying habits. For example, an auto company may identify four broad segments. Car buyers who are primarily seeking basic transportation or high performance or luxury or safety".[6] Depending upon the availability of man, material, financial and other resources companies have different ability to serve different segments of the market. Instead of trying to compete in an entire market, each company must identify the part of the market that it can serve best.

Since the buyers of a particular segment have similar wants, purchasing power and geographical location buying attitude and buying habits, it becomes easier for the marketers to develop their marketing plan for entering the segment. Here lies the importance of segmenting the market.

Bases for segmenting consumer market

Researchers have used two different approaches in segmenting the consumer market. Some researcher segments the market on the basis of geographic, demographic and psychographic variables and examine whether the different segments exhibit different need or product response. For example, researcher might examine the differing attitude of different occupational groups towards a particular brand of TV.

Other researchers segment the market on the basis of consumers response to benefits sought, use occasions, or brands and examine whether the consumers who purchased

Onida TV differ in their geographic, demographic and psychographic variations from those who purchased Sony TV. The major segmentation variables; geographic, demographic, psychographic and behavioural segmentation, as listed by Philip Kotler are given below:

i) *Geographic segmentation: Region*, city, density and climate

ii) *Demographic basis of segmentation*: Age, family life cycle, family size, gender, income, occupation, education, religion, race, social class and nationality

iii) *Psychological basis of segmentation*: Life style and personality.

iv) *Behavioural basis of segmentation:* Occasion, benefits, user status, user rate, loyalty status and attitude towards product.

Response or behaviour of different segments to the marketing stimuli and the external environment are different, but the responses of the same segment are similar. This knowledge will enable the marketers to chalk out appropriate marketing strategies for the segment they plan to enter.

Consumer Behaviour

Consumer behaviour in essence means buying behaviour. According to Philip Kotler and Garry Armstrong, "Consumer buying behaviour refers to the buying behaviour of final consumers - individuals and household who buy goods and services for personal consumption. All of these final consumers combined make up the consumer market".[7]

Leon G. Schiffman and Leslie Lazar Kanuk refer the study of consumer behaviour as "The study of how individuals make decisions to spend their available resources (time, money, and effort) on consumption related items. It includes the study of what they buy, why they buy it, when they buy it, where they buy it, how often they buy it and how often they use it". [8]

In a particular consumer market, "Consumer behaviour results from individual and environmental influences. Consumers often purchase goods and services which they want others to accept. Behaviour is, therefore, determined by the individual's psychological make up and the influence of others. The dual influence has been summarized in the following simplified equation of behaviour.

$$B = f(P,E)$$

Consumer behaviour (B) is, therefore, the result of the interaction of the consumer's personal influences (P) and the pressures exerted upon them by outside environment (E). Understanding consumers' behaviour requires that we understand the nature of these influences. The four basic determinants of consumer behaviour are the individual's needs, motives, perceptions, and attitudes. The interaction of these factors with the influences of the environment causes the consumer to act."[9]

For the purpose of the study, consumer behaviour refers to the response of the consumer as a result of the interaction of the personal influences and external influences, in terms of product choice, brand choice, dealer choice, purchase amount and purchase timing. A diagrammatic representation of the factors influencing the consumer behaviour is given in Figure 2 (Chapter 1).

Moreover, Philip Kotler has given a stimulus response model of Buyer behaviour as shown in the following figure 3.

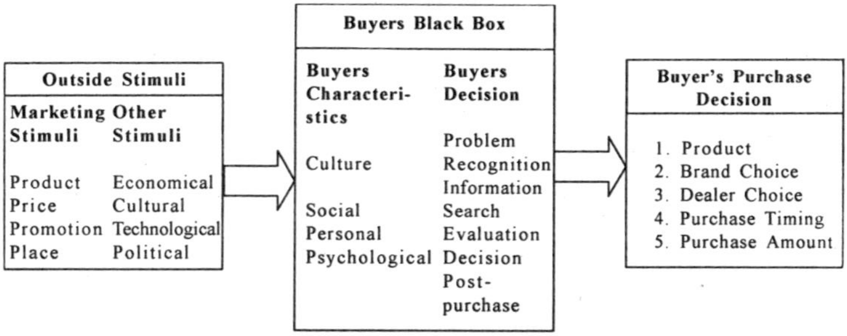

Figure: 3 Model of Buyer Behaviour[10]

"Marketing and environment stimuli enter the buyer's consciousness. The buyer's characteristics and decision process lead to certain purchase decisions. The marketer's task is to understand what happens in the buyer's consciousness between the arrival of outside stimuli and the buyers purchase decisions".[11]

Factors influencing the Consumer Behaviour

At a particular point of time, consumer has many needs. It may be biogenic such as hunger, thirst, etc. or/and psychogenic, such as need for recognition, esteem or belongingness. Consumer looks for products/services that can satisfy his needs.

A need becomes motives when it is sufficiently pressing to drive the consumer to purchase product/service. A motivated consumer is ready to act. How a motivated consumer purchase product/service is influenced by his perception about the buying situation.

A buying situation consists of marketing stimuli such as product, price, place and promotion offered by the marketers, surrounding environments consisting of Micro and macro environments and the individual consumer's personality or self concept.

Consumer's perception about a particular product/service as good enough to satisfy his need depends not only on the marketing stimuli but also on the stimuli's relation to surrounding and on the personality and self-concept of the individual consumer.

When he acts or purchases the product, he learns about the product. This leads to the consumer's belief about the product and consequently forms favourable or unfavourable attitudes towards the product. As a result consumer will behave consistently towards the similar product. Next time when he feels the same need he will buy the product towards which he has favourable attitude.

So understanding of the consumer behaviour requires the internalization of the basic determinants that influence the consumer behaviour.

The major factors that influence the consumer behaviour are:

a) The macro and the micro environmental factors, the external factors which indirectly influence the consumer behaviour.

b) Individual factors which directly influence the consumer.

Macro Environmental Factors

The general socio-economic conditions of the country referred to as macro environment indirectly influence the consumers.

For example, in 1991, Indian economy integrated with the economies of the world. Now there is no restriction (like quotas, licenses, high tariff, and administrative barrier) on the amount of product or factors that are exported or imported.

The proportion of import and export both in GNP for the year 1999-2001 is over 22%. Whereas prior to liberalization was 16% only in the year 1990-91.

As a result of liberalisation, Indian economy has benefited in manifold. It has improved the efficiency of the industry by resorting to the principle of "competitive advantage". It has increased the supplies of finance needed for growth and industrialization of a country. It has also enabled the domestic industries to reach to the international market.

To the general public, it has benefited in terms of availability of job opportunities and increase in salary. Thus, the disposable income of the people also has been increased. Consumers have benefited in terms of availability of the different brands including foreign brand of a product which they want to purchase. Now, they have a better option for the money they want to spend on the product.

Micro Environmental Factors

Some of the factors which come under this category are:

a) Culture

b) Sub-culture

c) Social class

d) Social group

e) Family

f) Personal

g) Others.

Culture

Culture has been defined as "the sum total of learned beliefs, values, and customs that serves to direct the consumer behaviour of members of a particular society".[12]

The consumer behaviour that is the thing they buy is influenced by the consumers' background or culture. Different emphasis is given by different cultures for buying, use, and disposing of products. People in the southern India have a certain style of consumption of food, clothing, saving etc. They differ from the people in the Northern India. A child growing up in the United States of America is exposed to the following culture and values; achievement and success, activity, efficiency, and productivity, progress, material comfort, individualism, freedom, external comfort, humanitarian and youthfullness. Consumers belonging to different culture behave differently. Therefore, in consumer behaviour culture plays a very important part.

Sub-culture

Leon G. Schiffinan and Leslie Lazar Kanuk[13] have defined sub-culture as a distinct cultural group that exists as an identifiable segment within a lager, more complex society. Within a culture there are many groups or segments of people with distinct customs, traditions and behaviour. In the Indian culture itself, there are many sub-cultures, the culture of the south, the north, east and the west, Hindu culture, Muslim culture. Hindus of the south differ in culture from the Hindus of the north. Products are designed to suit a target group of customers which have similar cultural backgrounds and are homogenous in many respects.

Social class

Social class is defined as the division of members of a society into a hierarchy of distinct status classes in such a manner that members of each class have relatively the same status and members of all other classes have either more or less status. Social class is defined by parameter like income, education, occupation, etc. Within a social class, people share the same value and beliefs and tend to purchase similar kinds of products.

Their choice of residence, type of laundry, entertainment, leisure all seems to be alike. The knowledge of social class and their customer behaviour is of great value to a marketer.

Social group

A group is a collection of individuals who share some consumer relationship, attitude, and have the same interest. Such groups are prevalent in societies. These groups could be primary where interaction takes place frequently and consists of family groups. These groups have a lot of interaction amongst them and are well-knit.

Secondary groups are a collection of individuals where relationship is more formal and less personal in nature. These could be political groups, walk groups, and study groups, service organisation like the Lions, Rotary etc. The behaviour of a group is influenced by other members of the group. An individual can be a member of various groups and can have varied influences by different members of groups in his consumption behaviour. An individual can be an executive in a company; can be a member of a political party. He may be a member of service organisation and of entertainment clubs and study circles. These exert different influences on his consumption.

Family influence

The family is the most important of primary group and is the strongest source of influence on consumer behaviour. The family tradition and customs are learnt by children and they imbibe many behavioural patterns from their family members, both consciously and unconsciously. These behaviour patterns become a part of children's lives. In a joint family many decision are jointly made which also leave an impression on the members of the family. These days the structure of the family is changing and people also going in more for nucleus families which consists of parent and dependent children. The other type of family is the joint family where mother, father, grandparents, and relatives are also living together.

Personal influence

A buyer's decision is also influenced by personal characteristics. This includes the buyer's age and stage in the life cycle, occupation, economic circumstances.

Age and stage in the life cycle

People buy different goods and service over a life time. They eat baby food in the early years, most foods in the growing and mature years and special diets in the later years. Taste in clothes, furniture and a recreation is also age related consumption and is shaped by the family life cycle. Nine stages of the family life cycle as listed by Philip Kotler are given below:

1. *Bachelor stage*: Young, single and not living at home.
2. *Newly married couples*: young and no children.
3. *Full nest I*: youngest child under six
4. *Full nest II*: youngest child six or over.
5. *Full nest III*: older married couple with dependent children
6. *Empty nest I*: older married couple, no children living with them, heads of the household in labour force.
7. *Empty nest II*: older married, no children living at home, head of household retired.
8. Solitary survivor in labour force
9. Solitary survivor, retired.

Marketers often choose life cycle groups in their target market.

Occupation and the economic circumstance

Occupation also influences a person's consumption

pattern. A blue-collar worker will buy work clothes, work shoes and lunch boxes. A company president will buy expensive suits, air travel, country club, membership and large sailboat. Marketers try to identify the occupational groups that have above average interest in their products and services. A company can even specialise its product for certain occupational groups.

Product choice is greatly affected by economic circumstances; spendable income savings and assets, debts, borrowing power, and attitude towards spending versus saving.

Marketers of income sensitive goods pay constant attention to trends in personal income, saving and interest rates. If economic indicators point to a recession, marketers can take step to redesign, reposition and re-price their product. So they continue to offer value to target customers.

Other influences

Martin Khan[14] reasons that consumers are also influenced by national or regional events which would be like the Asiad, the Olympics, Cricket test matches, World cup, the war or the calamity. These have permanent or temporary impression on the mind of the consumer and affect his behaviour.

In these events, products are advertised and sometimes the use of a product like drugs etc is discouraged. People are urged to adopt family planning methods. Situations variables such as product display, price reduction, free gifts, and attractive offers also influence consumer behaviour.

Individual factors

A person buying choice is influenced by five major psychological factors - *motivation, perception, learning, belief and attitude and personal and self-concept.*

Motivation

A person has many needs at any given time. Some needs are biogenic; they arise from physiological states of tension such as hunger, thirst, discomfort. Other needs are psychogenic; they arise from psychological states of tension such as the need of recognition, esteem and belonging. And need becomes a motive when it is arose to a sufficient level of intensity. A motive is a need that is sufficiently pressing to drive the person to act. Psychologists have developed theories of human motivation; three of the best known - the theories of Sigmund Freud, Abraham Maslow, and Frederick Herzberg—carry quite different implications for consumer analysis and strategy.

Perception

A motivated person is ready to act. How the motivated person actually acts is influenced by his or her perception of the situation. "Perception is the process by which an individual selects, organizes, and interprets information inputs to create a meaningful picture of the world".[15] Perception depends not only on the physical stimuli but also on the stimuli's relation to the surrounding field and on conditions within the individuals.

The key word in the definition of perception is individual one person might perceive a fast talking salesperson as aggressive and insincere; another as intelligent and hopeful. People can emerge with different perceptions of the same object because of three perceptual process; selective attention, selective distortion and selective retention.

Learning

When people act, they learn. Learning involves changes in an individual's behaviour arising from experience. Most human behaviour is learned. Learning theorist believe that learning is produced through interplay of desires, stimuli, cues, responses, and reinforcement.

Belief and Attitude

Through doing and learning people acquire belief and attitude. These in turn influence buying behaviour.

"A belief is a descriptive thought that a person holds about something".[16]

Belief may be based on knowledge, opinion or faith. They may or may not carry an emotional charge. Of course, manufactures are very interested in the beliefs people carry in their heads about their products and services. These beliefs make up product or brand images and people act on their images. If some beliefs are wrong and inhabit purchase, the manufacture will want to launch a campaign to correct these beliefs.

"An attitude is a person's enduring favourable or unfavourable evaluation, emotional feelings, and action tendencies towards some object or idea".[17]

People have attitudes towards almost everything—religion, politics, clothes, music, food, etc. Attitudes put them into a frame of mind of liking or disliking an object, moving towards or away from it. Attitude leads people to behave a fairly consistent way towards similar objects. People do not have to interpret and react to every object in a fresh way. Because attitude economise on energy and thought, they are very difficult to change. A person's attitudes settle into consistent pattern. To change a simple attitude may require major adjustments in other attitudes. Thus a company would be well advised to fit its product into existing attitudes rather than to try to change people's attitudes. Of course, there is exception where the cost of trying to change attitude might payoff.

Personality of self concept

Each person has a distinct personality that influence buying behaviour. By personality we mean distinguishing psychological characteristics that lead to relatively consistent and enduring responses to environment.

Keren Horney[18] proposed that individual can be classified into three personality groups: Compliant, Aggressive and Detached.

1. Compliant individuals are those who move towards other. They desire to be loved, wanted and appreciated.
2. Aggressive individuals are those who move against other. They desire to excel and win admiration.
3. Detached individuals are those who move away from others. They desire independence, self-reliance, self-sufficiency, and freedom from obligation.

Personality can be useful variable in analyzing consumer behaviour provided that personality type can be classified accurately and that strong correlations exist between certain personality types and product or brand choices.

For example, a computer company might discover that many prospects show high self-confidence, dominance, and autonomy. This suggests designing computer advertisements to appeal to these traits. Related to personality is self-concept or a self-image. Marketers try to develop the brand images that match the target markets self-image. It is possible that a person's actual self concept i.e. how she views herself differ from her ideal self concept i.e. how she would like to view herself and from her others self-concept i.e. how she thinks other see her. Which self will she try to satisfy in making a purchase? Because it is very difficult to answer this question, self-concept theory has had a mixed record of success in predicting consumer responses to brand image.

Buying Roles

Gary Armstrong and Philip Kotler reasons that the marketer needs to know what people are involved in the buying decision and what role each person plays.

For many products it is fairly easy to identify the buyer. Men normally choose tobacco and woman chooses their panty hose. On the other hand, other products involve a decision-making unit consisting of more than one person. Consider the selection of a family automobile. The suggestion to buy a new car might come from the oldest child. A friend might advise the family on the kind of car to buy. The husband might choose the make the wife might have definite desire regarding the car's appearance. The husband might take the final decision. The wife might end up using the car more than the husband does.

Thus five roles can be distinguished that the people might play in a buying decision.

i) *Initiator*; the person who first suggests or thinks of the idea of buying a particular product or service.

ii) *Influencer*; a person whose views or advice influences the buying decision.

iii) *Decider*; the person who ultimately makes a buying decision or any part of it - whether to buy, what to buy, how to buy or where to buy

iv) *Buyer*; the person who makes an actual purchase.

v) *User*; the person who consumes or uses a product or services.

A company needs to identify these roles because they have implications for designing the product, determining message, and allocating the promotional budget. If the husband decided on the car make, then the auto company will direct advertising to reach husbands. The auto company might design certain car features to please the wife. Knowing the main participants and their roles helps the marketer to develop appropriate marketing programme.

Types of Buying Behaviour

Consumer decision making varies with the types of buying-decision. There are great difference between buying tooth paste, a tennis racket, and a new car. Complex and expensive purchases are likely to involve more buyer deliberation and more participants. Assael distinguishes four types of consumer buying behaviour based on the degree of buyer involvement and the degree of difference among brands. These four types are:

i) *Complex buying behaviour* - High involvement and significant difference among the brands.

ii) *Dissonance reducing buying behaviour* - high involvement and few differences between brands.

iii) *Variety seeking buying behaviour*- low involvement and significance difference between brands.

iv) *Habitual buying behaviour* - low involvement and few differences between brands.

Consumer's Decision-making Process

A consumer passes through 5 stages in buying a product as suggested by Philip Kotler. The stages are problem recognition, information search. Evaluation of alternatives, purchase decision and post purchase behaviour (Fig. 4)

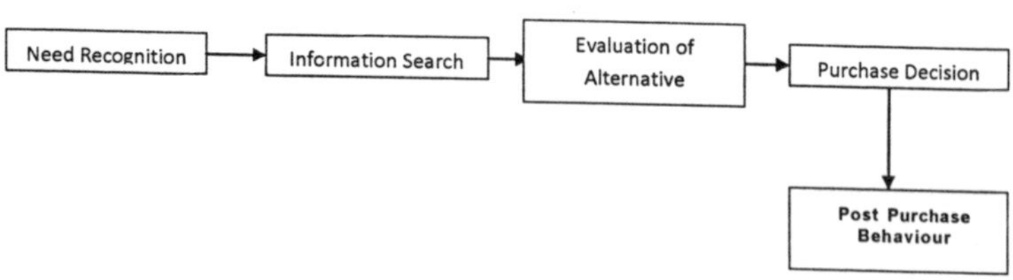

Figure 4: A Model of Decision-making Process

This particular model is more suitable to complex decision-making i.e. buying expensive and high involvement products. But for buying low involvement products, consumer may skip some of these stages. For example, a person buying his regular brand of toilet soap goes directly from the need of toilet soap to the purchase decision. Decision is made to solve the problem of any kind. The various stages in consumer decision-making are discussed as under:

Need / Problem recognition

A consumer may be having a need/problem. The decision process starts when the buyer recognizes the need. This need may be triggered by the external stimuli such as show room display and commercial advertisements. The marketer needs to identify the circumstances that trigger a particular need. By gathering information from a number of consumers, the marketer can identify the most frequent stimuli that spark an interest in a product category. The marketer can then develop marketing strategies that trigger consumer market.

Information search

On the second stage, information search is carried on by the consumer to find out how the need/problem can be solved. Consumer information sources fall in four groups:

(i) *Personal source*: family, friends, neighbours and acquaintances

(ii) *Commercial source*: Advertising, salespersons, dealers, packaging and displays

(iii) *Public source*: Mass media and consumer rating organisation

(iv) *Experiential sources*: Handling, examining and using the product.

The marketer should identify the consumer's information sources and evaluate their relative importance. The result will help company in the preparation of effective communication for the target market.

Evaluation of alternatives

At this stage, consumers evaluate the various alternatives that can solve his problem or satisfied his needs. Cost-benefit analysis is made to decide which product and brand image will be suitable or can take care of the problem suitable and adequately the consumer often looks for certain benefits/ attitudes from product solution. The marketer often segments the market according to the benefit sought by the consumers.

Purchase decision

Consumer after evaluating various alternatives forms preference among the brands and he also forms purchase intention to buy the most preferred brands. At this stage, two factors can intervene between the purchase intention and the purchase decisions. The first factor is the attitude of others. The extent to which another person's attitude reduces one's preferred alternative depends upon two things: the intensity of other person's negative attitude towards the consumer's preferred alternative and the consumer's motivation to comply with other person's wishes.

The more intense the other person's negativism and the closer the other person are to the consumer, the more the consumer will adjust his purchase intention. A buyer's preference for a brand will increase if some one he likes favour the same brand. Purchase intention is also influenced by unanticipated situational factors. The consumer forms a purchase intention on the basis of such factors as expected family income, expected price, and expected product benefits. When the consumer is about to act, unanticipated situational factors may erupt to change the purchase intention. A consumer who decides to execute a purchase intention will be making five purchase sub-decisions:

(i) Brand decision
(ii) Quantity decision
(iii) Dealer decision
(iv) Timing decision and
(v) Payment method.

But the purchase of daily used products involves fewer decisions. For example, in buying toilet soap, a consumer give little thought to the dealer and payment methods.

Post-purchase behaviour

Consumer after constant use of the product leads to the satisfaction or dissatisfaction of the consumer, which leads to repeat purchases, or to the rejection of the product. Marketer can take steps to minimise the amount of consumer post-purchase dissatisfaction. It is also important for the marketer to monitor how the buyer uses and dispose of the product. If the consumer finds a new use of the product, this can be of very interesting to the marketer. If the consumer resale the product, this will reduce the new sales of the product. If they throw the product away, how it is disposed of is very important to the marketer because the product may deteriorate the environment.

Understanding consumer's decision-making process is very important to the marketer for developing effective marketing strategies to meet the needs of the consumer or to solve the problems of the consumer.

Four Views of Consumer Decision-making

Consumer's decision-making can be examined in terms of the following four views as given by Leon G. Schiffinan and Leslie, Lazar Kanuk.

An economic view

This view has its root in "economic man" model. According

to this view, consumer takes rational decision. Rational decision implies that consumers are aware of all the product alternatives, capable of correctly ranking each alternatives in terms of benefits and advantages and able to identify the best alternative one.

But this view has been criticized for the following reasons: people are limited by their existing skills and habits, people are limited by their existing values and goals and people are limited by the extent of their knowledge.

A passive view

A passive view portrays consumer as an irrational and impulsive purchaser. Consumers are submissive to the promotional efforts of the marketer. Consumers can be easily taken away by advertisement and skill full presentation of the salesmen. This view considers consumer as an object that can be manipulated. This view has been criticized because it fails to recognise that consumer plays an equal role in many buying situations. Consumers do have motivation, selective perception, & communication which serve to support the propositions that consumers are rarely object of manipulation

A cognitive view

This view perceives consumers as a thinking problem solver. Consumers actually search for products or services that fulfill their needs and enrich their lives. Consumer seeks and evaluates information about selected brands and retail outlets. The cognitive view describes a consumer who falls somewhere between the extremes of the economic and the passive view, who do not have total knowledge about available product alternatives and therefore can not make perfect decisions, but who nonetheless actively seeks information and attempts to make satisfactory decision.

An emotional view

According to this view, consumer's purchases are

associated with deep feelings or emotions such as joy, fear, love, hope, sexuality and fantasy. Consumers are likely to have many purchases on impulse or on whim or because they are emotionally driven rather than carefully searching and evaluating the information before buying.

Hence, depending upon the type of consumer decision making that is involved in a particular buying situation, marketer can develop an appropriate marketing plan for targeting the consumer.

Approaches to Studying Consumer Behaviour

Assael[19] outlines two broad approaches to the study of consumer behaviour. They are managerial approach and holistic approach.

The managerial approach views consumer behaviour as an applied social science and it is studied as a supplement to and a basis for developing marketing strategies. A holistic approach views consumer behaviour as pure social science and it focuses on enquiry without necessarily being considered for application.

A managerial approach

A managerial approach to consumer behaviour tends to be more micro and cognitive in nature. It is micro in the sense that it emphasises on the individual consumer; his attitude, perception, lifestyle and demographic characteristics. Environmental effects such as reference groups, family, and culture are studied in the context of how they influence the individual consumer. It is cognitive in the sense that it emphasises on the thought process of individual consumers and the factors that go into influencing their decisions. Managers on the basis of the information regarding the consumer needs, thought process, and characteristics identify the segment that can be targeted with the company's offerings to satisfy the needs of individual consumers in a socially responsible manner.

A holistic approach

A holistic approach is macro in its orientation in the sense that it focuses more in the nature of consumption experience rather than on the purchasing process. It stresses on the culturally derived context on consumption. For example: purchase of a product for giving gift to someone is culture-derived. A holistic approach is more interested in understating the environmental context of the consumer's action whereas a managerial approach is more interested in predicting what the consumer might do in future. This research focuses on both the approaches to unfold culture-related purchase decision and to develop appropriate marketing strategies to suit the consumer of Manipur.

Current Trend in Consumer Behaviour

As the environment where the consumer finds himself today is changing, his behaviour towards the product / service is also changing.

As per Henry Assael,[20] USA in the mid 1990s could witness important consumer behaviour trend. In particular, there are three significant trends that have influenced companies marketing strategies. There is a greater value orientation on the part of consumers, a desire for and access to more information and a desire for more customised products to fit in their needs.

Steep recession in the 1980s and 1990s has made consumers more price sensitive. Consumers are viewing price more in the context of values i.e., worth for the money they spend. Consumers are becoming more sensitive to value for the money they spend and this has led companies to keep price down without sacrificing quality of the product. Moreover, companies have started giving more emphasis on total quality management programmes. National marketers make product lines with both premium priced and lower priced brands. Consumers are becoming more aware and self-assured buyers. One reason is the greater accessibility of information and the availability of various options. The expansion of cable TV channels and home computers has expanded the availability of product information. With the increasing educational level of consumers, these additional information sources are likely to be used by the consumer in the decision-making. The greater sophistication, access to more information and emphasis on value have led consumers to desire products more closely fitted to their needs. Consumers today are looking for more options at lower price.

Consumer-oriented View of Marketing Strategy

The marketing concept which was formulated in 1950s philosophises that the marketing strategy that is to be developed for a market should be on the basis of the knowledge of the consumers. The marketing concept states that "the key to achieving organisational goal consists in determining the needs and wants of target markets and delivering the desired satisfactions more effectively and efficiently than competitors".[21] Every organisation has financial objectives i.e., economic objectives. Organisation often looks for specific long run rate of return on investment and will know the profit that it would like to achieve in the current year. These financial objectives are usually converted into marketing objectives. For example, if the company wants to earn Rs. 1,800,000 profit and its target profit market is 10% on sales, then it must set a goal of Rs.18,000,000. in sales revenue. If the company sets an average price of Rs. 260, it must sell 69,230 units. For achieving this sale, the company will have to set certain goals for consumer awareness, distribution coverage and so on.

For achieving this marketing objectives, company should formulate the appropriate marketing strategy i.e., product strategy, pricing strategy, place strategy, and promotion strategy for the target consumers.

Product strategy calls for taking decision on product quality, design features, branding and packaging. Pricing strategy is related with the decision of wholesale and retail prices, discount, allowances and credit terms. Place strategy is related with the decision of various activities the company undertakes to make the product easily accessible and available to target consumer. And promotion strategy is related with the decisions of various activities the company undertake to communicate the products merit and to persuade target customers to buy them. The marketing concept seems so logical in today's marketing scenario that many wonder why marketers did not follow it prior to 1950s.

According to Henry Assael,[22] there are basically two main reasons:

First, marketing institutions are not fully developed before 1950 to accept the marketing concept. The implementation of the marketing concept requires a diversity of facilities for promoting and distributing products that meet the needs of smaller and more diverse market segments. This diversity in marketing institutions did not exist before 1950. In those days, the emphasis was on economies of scale in production and marketing.

The second reason is that there was no economic necessity to follow marketing concept. There was little purchasing power to spur on interest in consumer behaviour. There was no competitive pressure to discover consumer's motive or to adjust product offering to consumer needs. Manufacturers could sell whatever they made.

In the early 1950s, different marketers brought out similar lines of refrigerators, cars, etc. but then they found consumers reluctant to buy. Consumers had become more selective in their purchasing habits after two major wars and a depression and they had become reluctant buyers. The economy experienced its first true buyers market. For the first time supply exceeds demands and inventories build up in the face of consumer's purchasing power. Some marketers reacted with more foresight by recognizing that the right combination of product benefits would influence reluctant consumer to purchase. These manufacturers research the market to identify consumer needs and to develop products to fit those needs. This new approach resulted in an expanded set of product offerings.

Marketers began talking in behaviour terms. In this new approach, a product must be positioned to deliver a set of benefits to a defined segment of consumers. Thus, a shift to a consumer-oriented approach to marketing by business organisation has changed the nature of marketing operation by:

1. Providing a spur to consumer behaviour research.
2. Creating a more customer-oriented framework for marketing strategies.
3. Encouraging measurement of the factors that influence consumer to purchase.
4. Emphasising market segmentation.
5. Emphasising product positioning to meet consumer needs.
6. Creating greater selectivity in advertising and personal selling.
7. Creating more selective media and distribution outlets.

In short, in accepting the marketing concept, organisation has recognised that the determinants of consumer behaviour have a direct bearing on the formulation of marketing strategies.

NOTES

1. Schiffman, Leon G and Kanuk, Leslie Lazar, *Consumer Behaviour,* 6th Edition, Prentice Hall of India, 1997, p. 7.
2. Mehta, P.L., *Managerial Economics,* 6th edition, Sultan Chand & Sons Publication, 1993, p. 271.
3. Mehta, P.L., *op.cit.*, p. 271.
4. *Ibid.*, p. 271.
5. Kotler, Philip and Armstrong Gary, *Principles of Marketing,* 9th edition, Prentice Hall of India, 2001, p. 12.
6. Kotler, Philip, *Marketing Management,* 10th Edition, Prentice Hall of India, Sept, 1999, pp. 256-257.
7. Kotler, Philip and Armstrong Gary, *op.cit.,* p. 143.
8. Schiffman, Leon G and Kink, Leslie Lazar, *Consumer Behaviour,* 6th Edition, Prentice Hall of India, 1997, p. 6.
9. Rather, B.S., *Advertising Management,* 1st Edition, Himalaya & Publishing House, New Delhi, Reprint, 1990, p. 71.
10. Kotler, Philips, *op.cit.*, p. 164.
11. Kotler, Philips, *Marketing Management,* 10th Edition, Prentice Hall of India, Sept, 1999, p. 20.
12. Schiff man, Leon G and Kink, Leslie Lazar, *op.cit.*, p. 406.
13. *Ibid.*, p. 440.
14. Khan, Martin, *Consumer Behaviour,* New Age International Publishers, 2001, p. 22.
15. Kotler, Philip, *Marketing Management,* 7th Edition, Prentice Hail of India, 1991, p. 176.
16. *Ibid.*, p. 177.
17. *Ibid.*, p. 177.
18. Schiffman, Leon G and Kanuk, Leslie Lazar, *op.cit.*, pp. 123-125.
19. Assae1, Henry, *Consumer Behaviour,* 6th Edition, Asian Books Pvt. Ltd., 1998, p. 21.
20. *Ibid.*, p. 13.
21. Kotler, Philips, *op.cit.*, p. 16.
22. Assael, Henry, *op.cit.*, p. 8.

3

Present Scenario of Consumer Markets of Manipur

Introduction

Consumer market refers to the set of all actual or potential buyers who purchase products or services for personal consumption or for household uses.

A consumer market of a particular product has certain characteristics the knowledge of which is very important to the marketers for the formulation of appropriate marketing strategies.

The present chapter is an endeavour to depict the consumer market of Manipur with special reference to consumer non-durable goods *(Toilet Soap)* and consumer durable goods *(TV)* in certain aspects which are relevant to the purpose of the present study.

This chapter is divided into two parts. The first part describes the consumer market of consumer non-durable goods *(Toilet Soap)* and the second part presents the consumer market of durable goods *(TV)*.

Consumer Market of Non-durable Goods (Toilet Soap)

Tangible goods that normally are consumed in one or

few uses are called non-durable goods. Example of such products includes toilet soap, toothpaste, shampoo etc.

Toilet soap has become an essential household item in everyone's day to day life. It is important for the marketers of toilet soap to understand the characteristics of market so that they can chalk out appropriate marketing strategies for the satisfaction of consumers' needs and wants and accomplishment of objectives of the business organisations. For understanding the consumer market of Manipur with special reference to non-durable goods (toilet soap), the following aspects are discussed in this chapter.

i) Important marketers of toilet soap whose products are presently available in Manipur.

ii) Households using one or more brands of toilet soap.

iii) Average family size of the households.

iv) Usage rate of toilet soap.

v) Monthly average number of pieces of toilet soap consumption per household.

vi) Consumers using a particular brand of toilet soap for a particular period of time.

vii) Market shares of toilet soap.

viii) Household's and individual consumer's monthly average pieces of consumption, volumes of consumption of toilet soap and monthly average expenditure on toilet soap.

ix) Estimated monthly total consumption of toilet soap and monthly total expenditure on toilet soap in Manipur.

x) Per capita consumption of toilet soap in Manipur and in all India. Share of Manipur toilet soap market by volume in the Indian domestic market in the year 2001.

xi) Share of Manipur toilet soap market by value in the Indian domestic market in the year 2001.

1. Important marketers of Toilet Soap whose products are presently available in Manipur

There are as many as 38 brands of toilet soap which are presently available in Manipur market. Hindustan Lever Limited has the largest range of brands, as many as 10 brands with different varieties. Details of important brands of toilet soap are presented in Table 1.

Table 1

Important marketers of toilet soap whose products are available in Manipur and their brands, varieties, sizes and MRP of Toilet Soaps

Marketers	*Brand Names*	*Varieties*	*Sizes (gm)*	*MRP (Rs)*
I. Godrej Consumer Product Ltd		Lime Fresh	75	10.50
			125	15.50
		International	75	12.50
	Cinthol	Spice	75	13.50
		Deodorant	100	16.50
		Cologne	75	12.50
		Skin Fresh	75	9.50
		International	3x75	28.00
	No 1	Beauty Soap	75	6.50
		Rose	4x75	22.50
	Fair Glow		100	10.00
			75	11.50

(Contd....)

Marketers	*Brand Names*	*Varieties*	*Sizes (gm)*	*MRP (Rs)*
II. Proctor & Gamble Ltd	Camay	Natural	150	27.00
		Classic	150	31.00
III. Reckitt . Benckiser (India) Ltd	Dettol	Original	75	14.00
		Glycerin	75	18.00
		Original	2x75	24.00
IV. Hindustan Lever Ltd.		International	75	14.00
		White	100	10.00
	Lux	Skin Care	75	16.00
		Rich &	100	12.00
		Nourishing	50	5.00
		Active Red	125	9.50
		Plain	150	8.50
	Lifebuoy	Plus	100	10.00
		Gold	75	9.50
		Active Orange	100	8.00
	Liril	Lime Fresh	75	13.50
		Icy Cole Mint	75	16.00
	Pears		75	18.50
	Rexona		100	10.00
		Coconut Milk	100	11.50
	Ayush		75	9.50
		Rose	75	5.00
		Sandal	100	8.00
		2 in 1	100	8.50
	Breeze		50	5.00
		Lime	4x75	22.00
		Rose	4x100	27.00
		Sandal	4x75	22.00

(Contd....)

Marketers	*Brand Names*	*Varieties*	*Sizes (gm)*	*MRP (Rs)*
	Fair & Lovely		75	15.00
	Hamam	Herbal Skin	100	8.00
		Care	100	10.00
			50	4.50
	Savlon		75	15.00
(Imported & Marketed by Hindustan Lever Ltd)	Dove		100	45.00
V. Colgate Palmolive India Ltd.	Palmolive Natural	Extra Care	100	17.00
			75	14.00
		Natural	75	8.00
VI. Calcutta Chemicals	Aramusk	For men	75	15.00
VII. Johnson & Johnson Ltd.	Johnson Baby Soap		75	23.00
VIII. Dorcas Market Makers Ltd., Chennai	Medimix		75	10.00
IX. Nahar Industries, Ludhiana	Margo		75	13.00
X. Aura Oil Industries	Neem		100	11.50
XI. VVF Ltd.	Fa	Aqua	75	15.00
		Caribbean Lemon	75	15.00
		Exotic Garden	75	15.00

(Contd....)

Marketers	*Brand Names*	*Varieties*	*Sizes (gm)*	*MRP (Rs)*
XII. J.K. Halene Curtis Ltd.	Denim		100	14.00
			150	25.00
XIII. Nirma Ltd.	Nirma	Lime	100	8.00
			100	7.50
			3x100	22.00
		Sandal	3x100	20.00
XIV. Sangam Export, New Delhi	Fresh Soap	Glycerin	75	16.90
XV. Kamatka Soaps & Detergent Ltd.	Mysore Sandal	Skin Care	150	30.00
XVI. Cusson (International) Ltd., England	Beauty		75	9.50
			80	No MRP
			100	11.00
XVII. GYI Industries Ltd. Myanmar	Flower		70	No MRP
XVIII. United Pacific Co. Ltd., Myanmar	Paris	Fresh Soap	90	No MRP
		Aloe Vera	90	No MRP
		Cucumber	90	No MRP
	Fresh Soap	Honey	70	No MRP
		Cucumber	90	No MRP
		Jasmine	90	No MRP
		UV Protection	90	No MRP
XIX. PT Sayap Mas Utama Jakarta, Indonesia	GIV		80	No MRP
XX. Elan Co.	Rose		75	No MRP

Note 1: *Less known brands such as Imperial Leather, Jai, Nikhar, Clinics are not included in the above list.*

Note 2: *Brands having no MRP tag are sold between Rs. 8.00 and Rs. 10.00*

2. Households using one or more brands of toilet soap

Some households, in general, use only one brand of toilet soap irrespective of the family size. But, some households use two or more brands of toilet soap. Information gathered from 752 households in this aspect is presented in Table 2.

Table 2
Households using single brand, two brands, three brands, and four brand of Toilet Soap

	No. of Households – District-wise						
No of Brands	*Bishnupur*	*Thoubal*	*Imphal East*	*Imphal West*	*Church-andpur*	*Total*	*Per-centage*
a. Only One brand	99	87	123	96	68	473	62.89
b. Two brands	38	30	14	49	20	151	20.07
c. Three brands	15	26	8	24	2	75	9.97
d. Four brands	21	8	6	10	8	53	7.04
Total	173	151	151	179	98	752	100

It is seen from the above table that majority of the households i.e. 62.89% of the households covered for the study use only one brand of toilet soap whereas 20.07%, 9.97% and 7.04% of the households use two, three and four brands of toilet soap respectively. Further, among the districts, Imphal East district has the highest percentage of households using only one brand of toilet soap with 81.45% (123 out of 151 households). This is followed by Churchandpur district with 69.38% (68 out of 98 households) of the households using only one brand of toilet soap.

3. Average family size of the households

Information regarding the family size of the households covered for the study is given in Table 3.

Table 3
Households having a particular Family Size

Family Size (No of Family Members)	*No of Households – District-wise*					
	Bishnupur	*Thoubal*	*Imphal East*	*Imphal West*	*Churchandpur*	*Total*
2 (Two)	1		4	4	2	11
3 (Three)	3	10	10	10	4	37
4 (Four)	11	18	28	32	19	108
5 (Five)	31	38	48	49	24	190
6 (Six)	33	37	27	38	22	157
7 (Seven)	44	23	21	19	16	123
8 (Eight)	16	14	10	11	5	56
9 (Nine)	12	3	2	4	2	23
10 (Ten)	8	5	1	7	1	22
11 (Eleven)	3	1		2	1	7
12 (Twelve)	6	1		2	2	11
13 (Thirteen)	3					3
14 (Fourteen)	1			1		2
15 (Fifteen)		1				1
16 (Sixteen)	1					1
Total	173	151	151	179	98	752

Average Family Size

Information from Table 3 is used for the calculation of average family size of the households of Manipur.

Table 4
Worksheet for the calculation of average family size of the households

Family Size (x)	*No of Households (f)*	*fx*	*Average Family Size*
2 (Two)	11	22	
3 (Three)	37	111	
4 (Four)	108	432	
5 (Five)	190	950	
6 (Six)	157	942	
7 (Seven)	123	861	Arithmetic Mean= $\frac{\Sigma fx}{\Sigma f}$
8 (Eight)	56	448	
9 (Nine)	23	207	= 4500 ÷ 752 = 5.98 ≅ 6(Approx)
10 (Ten)	22	220	
11 (Eleven)	7	77	
12 (Twelve)	11	132	
13 (Thirteen)	3	39	
14 (Fourteen)	2	28	
15 (Fifteen)	1	15	
16 (Sixteen)	1	16	
Total	752	4500	

It is observed from the above table that the average family size of the households of Manipur is 6 persons (approximately).

4. Usage rate of Toilet Soap

Different persons have different usage rate of toilet soap. There is also difference in the usage rate between male and female. Information in this regard is presented in the following Table 5.

Table 5
Daily usage rate of Toilet Soap

UsageRate	*No of respondents - district & gender wise*															*Total*		*Overall Total*
	Bishnupur			*Thoubal*			*Imphal East*			*Imphal West*			*Churchandpur*					
	M	*F*	*T*	*M*	*F*	*T*	*M*	*F*	*T*	*M*	*F*	*T*	*M*	*F*	*T*	*M*	*F*	
1 time				3		3	14		14	7	2	9				24	2	26
2 times	36	14	50	59	9	68	52	18	70	51	12	63	21	7	28	219	60	279
3 times	59	27	86	38	9	47	36	11	47	55	12	67	27	10	37	215	69	284
4 times	19	9	28	19	10	29	13	5	18	14	9	23	13	12	25	78	45	123
5 times	6	1	7	4		4	2		2	2	3	5	4	2	6	18	6	24
6 times		1	1							6	1	7	1	1	2	7	3	10
7 times		1	1							2	3	5				2	4	6
Total	120	53	173	123	28	151	117	34	151	137	42	179	66	32	98	563	189	752

Note: M, F and T stand for Male, Female and Total respectively.

Daily usage rate of Toilet Soap

Information given in Table 5 is used for the determination of average usage rate of male, female and a person.

Table 6
Worksheet for the calculation of average usage rate of toilet soap of male, female and a person

Daily usage rate x	*No of Males f_1*	*No of Females f_2*	*Overall Totals f_3*	f_1x	f_2x	f_3x
1 time	24	2	26	24	2	26
2 times	219	60	279	438	120	558
3 times	215	69	284	645	207	852
4 times	78	45	123	312	180	492
5 times	18	6	24	90	30	120
6 times	7	3	10	42	18	60
7 times	2	4	6	14	28	42
Total	563	189	752	1565	585	2150

Here,
Average usage rate of Male $= \Sigma (f_1x)/ \Sigma (f_1) = 1565/563 = 2.77$
Average usage rate of Female $= \Sigma (f_2x)/ \Sigma (f_2) = 585/189 = 3.09$
Average usage of a Person $= \Sigma (f_3x)/ \Sigma (f_3) = 2150/752 = 2.85$

It is observed that the daily usage rate of female is greater than that of male. Further, daily usage rate of toilet soap of a person is 3 times approximately.

5. Monthly average number of pieces of toilet soap consumption per household

Different households consumed different number of pieces of toilet soap. Monthly number of pieces of toilet soap consumed by different households of Manipur is given in Table 7.

Table 7
Households consuming a particular number of pieces of Toilet Soap per month

Family Size (No of Family Members)	*No of Households – District-wise*					
	Bishnupur	*Thoubal*	*Imphal East*	*Imphal West*	*Churchandpur*	*Total*
2 (Two)	3	21	9	15	10	58
3 (Three)	14	35	18	10	16	93
4 (Four)	23	17	23	22	12	97
5 (Five)	27	20	26	33	20	126
6 (Six)	28	24	33	27	10	122
7 (Seven)	22	14	12	33	12	93
8 (Eight)	15	8	14	18	2	57
9 (Nine)	17	6	5	6	7	41
10 (Ten)	10	2	5	4	4	25
11 (Eleven)	6	1	2	4	1	14
12 (Twelve)	4	1	2	3	2	12
13 (Thirteen)	2	1	1	1	2	7
14 (Fourteen)	1	1	1	1		4
15 (Fifteen)	1			2		3
Total	173	151	151	179	98	752

Information given in the Table 7 is used in the determination of the monthly average number of pieces of toilet soap consumption per household.

Table 8
Worksheet for the calculation of monthly average number of pieces of toilet soap consumption per household

Number of Pieces consumed (x)	*No of households (f)*	*Fx*	*Monthly average number of pieces of consumption per Household*
2	58	116	
3	93	279	
4	97	388	
5	126	630	
6	122	732	
7	93	651	
8	57	456	Arithmetic Mean= $\frac{\Sigma fx}{\Sigma f}$
9	41	369	
10	25	250	=4361/752
11	14	154	=5.799 ≅6(Approx)
12	12	144	
13	7	91	
14	4	56	
15	3	45	
Total	752	4361	

6. Consumers using a particular brand of toilet soap for a particular period of time

In general some consumers do not stick to a particular brand of toilet soap for a longer period of time owing to one reason or other. Consumers usually switch to another brand just because the brand which they have been using does not meet their expectations or the consumers want to try others brands available in the market. But, a satisfied consumer tends to use a particular brand for a longer period of time and later they become a loyal consumer of the brand. In this regard, information is gathered and presented in the following Table 9.

Table 9
Consumers using a particular brand of toilet soap for a particular period of time

Time Period	*No of Persons – District-wise Total*					
	Bishnupur	*Thoubal*	*Imphal East*	*Imphal West*	*Churchandpur*	*Total*
1 month	5	2	29	3	1	40
2 months	13	1	9	3	7	33
3 months	14	1	10	4	5	34
4 months	7	4	3		1	15
5 months	11	2	2	3	1	19
6 months	3	14	4	4	1	26
7 months	3	1		1		5
8 months						
9 months	1					1
10 months	2					2
11 months						
1 year	18	9	11	18	20	76
2 years	33	31	20	45	29	158
3 years	20	13	11	29	6	79
4 years	8	8	2	11	5	34
5 years	12	10	10	20	7	59
6 years	2	3	6	3	1	15
7 years	3	15	3	3	3	27
8 years		1	1			2
9 years		2	1		1	4
10 years	5	10	9	7	3	34
11 years		1	3	5		9
12 years	1	8	8	3	2	22
13 years	1	1		1		3
14 years	1	1				2
15 years	3	3	1	1	1	9
16 years			2			2
1 7 years			5			5
18 years		1				1
19 years	1					1
20 years	2	2		7		11
Childhood	4	7	1	8	4	24
Total	173	151	151	179	98	752

It is seen from the above table that majority of the respondents (76.72% i.e., 577 out of 752 respondents) have been using the brand which they are presently using for one year or more. This indicates that majority of the consumers of Manipur are brand loyal consumers.

7. Market shares of Toilet Soaps

For determining the market shares of each brand, market share of each size of toilet soap and market share of price range of toilet soap, information regarding monthly consumption of number of pieces of toilet soap size-wise by 752 households covered for the study is presented in the following Table 10.

Table 10

Brand and size-wise consumption of Toilet Soap per month by the sampled households

Brands	*No. of Pieces– District-wise*						
	Size (gm)	*Bishnupur*	*Thoubal*	*Imphal East*	*Imphal West*	*Church-andpur*	*Total*
1. Cinthol	75	105	65	21	111	36	338
	100	39	50	58	56	19	222
	125	7	5	4	8	6	30
2. Lux	50	6	4	3	4	6	23
	75	27	74	101	116	26	344
	100	28	40	42	34	27	171
3. Beauty	75	78	17	10	16	6	127
	80	68	50	80	25	26	249
	100	83	32	80	29	46	270
4. Lifebouy	75	54	20	23	27	53	177
	100	34	4	66	26	30	197
	125	5	1	4	5	5	22
	150	7	34	5	6	3	25
5. Liril	75	53	53	108	42	42	298
6. Nirma	100	57	85	26	33	29	230

(Contd....)

Brands	Size (gm)	No. of Pieces– Districtwise: Bishnupur	Thoubal	Imphal East	Imphal West	Churchandpur	Total
7. Rexona	100	60	29	37	58	29	213
8. Breeze	50	5	4	3	4	3	19
	75	72	29	11	13	6	131
	100	15	5	14	12	5	51
9. Dove	100	14		24	91	26	155
10. Palmolive	75	12	15	13	59	8	107
	100	6	28	22	21	5	82
11. Pears	75	8	11	42	51	30	142
12. Paris	90	83	26		11	3	123
13. No 1	75	73	10			13	96
14. Margo	75	31	9	11	72		123
15. GIV	80	16			5	27	48
16. Savlon	75	18	3		17		38
17. Dettol	75	16		24	29		69
18. Camay	150	8	2	7	27		44
19. Rose	50	7	8			7	22
20. Hamam	50		4	3	4		11
	100		8	5	12		25
21. Fa	75		2		9	5	16
22. MediMix	75	5			13		18
23. Neem	100			9	8		17
24. Others	50	4					4
	70	4			10	3	7
	75	20	9		14	3	42
	100	8			3	7	29
	150	3					6
Total		1139	745	856	1081	540	4361

Notes: 1 Others include 15 less used brands. They are Ayush, Marvel, Nikhar, Denim, Clinics, Johnson & Johnson Baby, Fair & Lovely, Flower, Park Avenue, Jai, Imperial Leather, Natural, Fresh, Fair Glow and Sanifresh.

2 There are 5 households which use Amway products of 250 ml bottle each per month apart from using other bar soaps.

Market shares of Toilet Soap Brands by volume (gm.)

With the help of the information given in the *Table. 10*, market shares of different brands of toilet soap by volume are given in the Table 11.

Table 11
Worksheet for the calculation of market shares of toilet soap brands by volume (gm.) of consumption

Brand	*Size in gm(a)*	*Total no of piece(b)*	*Size-wise volume in gm (a x b)*	*Brand Wise total volume (Km)*	*Market Share (%)*
1	*2*	*3*	*4*	*5*	*6*
1. Cinthol	75	338	25350		
	100	222	22200	51300	13.54
	125	30	3750		
2. Lux	50	23	1150		
	75	344	25800	44050	11.63
	100	171	17100		
3. Beauty	75	127	9525		
	80	249	19920	56445	14.90
	100	270	27000		
4. Lifebouy	75	177	13275		
	100	197	19700		
	125	22	2750	39475	10.42
	150	25	3750		
5. Liril	75	298	22350	22350	5.90
6. Nirma	100	230	23000	23000	6.07
7. Rexona	100	213	21300	21300	5.62
8. Breeze	50	19	950		
	75	131	9825	15875	4.19
	100	51	5100		
9. Dove	100	155	15500	15500	4.09
10. Palmolive	75	107	8025		
	100	82	8200	16225	4.28

(Contd....)

1	2	3	4	5	6
11. Pears	75	142	10650	10650	2.81
12. Paris	90	123	11070	11070	2.92
13. No 1	75	96	7200	7200	1.90
14. Margo	75	123	9225	9225	2.43
15. GIV	80	48	3840	3840	1.01
16. Savlon	75	38	2850	2850	0.75
17. Dettol	75	69	5175	5175	1.36
18. Camay	150	44	6600	6600	1.74
19. Rose	75	22	1650	1650	0.43
20. Hamam	50	11	550		
	100	25	2500	3050	0.80
21. Fa	75	16	1200	1200	0.31
22. MediMix	75	18	1350	1350	0.35
23. Neem	100	17	1700	1700	0.44
24. Others	50	4	200		
	70	7	490		
	75	42	3150	7640	2.01
	100	29	2900		
	150	6	900		
Total		4361		378720	100.00

It is observed from Table 11 that the first three brands which occupy the highest shares of market by volume (gm.) of toilet soap consumption per month are *Beauty, Cinthol and Lux* with *14.9%, 13.54%* and *11.63%* of total market respectively.

Market shares of toilet soap brands by value (Rupee). With the help of the information given in the Table 1 and Table 10, market shares of toilet soap brands by value (Rupees) are determined as shown in the Table 12.

Table 12
Worksheet for the calculation of market shares of toilet soap brands by value

Brand Name	*Size (gm)*	*No of pieces consumed (a)*	*MRP/AVG MRP of same size (b) Rs*	*Size-Wise value (a x b) Rs*	*Brand-Wise total value Rs*	*Market Share %*
1	*2*	*3*	*4*	*5*	*6*	*7*
1. Cinthol	75	338	11. 70	3954.6		
	100	222	16.5	3663	8082.6	14.35
	125	30	15.5	465		
2. Lux	50	23	5.00	115		
	75	344	15.00	5160	7156	12.70
	100	171	11.00	1881		
3. Beauty	75	127	9.50	1206.5		
	80	249	10.00	2490	6666.5	11.84
	100	270	11.00	2970		
4. Lifebouy	75	177	7.50	1327.5		
	100	197	9.00	1773	3522	6.25
	125	22	9.50	209		
	150	25	8.50	212.5		
5. Liril	75	298	14.75	4395.5	4395.5	7.88
6. Nirma	100	230	7.75	1782.5	1782.5	3.16
7. Rexona	100	213	11.75	2502.75	2502.75	4.44
8. Breeze	50	19	5.00	95		
	75	131	5.00	655	1170.75	2.07
	100	51	8.25	420.75		
9. Dove	100	155	45.00	6975	6975	12.38
10. Palmolive	75	107	11.00	1177	2571	4.56
	100	82	17.00	1394		
11. Pears	75	142	18.5	2627	2627	4.66
12. Paris	90	123	9.00	1107	1107	1.96

(Contd....)

1	2	3	4	5	6	7
13. No 1	75	96	6.5	624	624	1.10
14. Margo	75	123	13.00	1599	1599	2.83
15. GIV	80	48	9.00	432	432	0.76
16. Savlon	75	38	15.00	570	570	1.01
17. Dettol	75	69	16.00	1104	1104	1.96
18. Camay	150	44	29.00	1276	1276	2.26
19. Rose	75	22	9.00	198	198	0.35
20. Hamam	50	11	4.50	49.5	274.5	0.48
	100	25	9.00	225		
21. Fa	75	16	15.00	240	240	0.42
22. MediMix	75	18	10.00	180	180	0.31
23. Neem	100	17	11.50	195.5	195.5	0.34
24. Others	50	4	5.00	20		
	70	7	8.00	56		
	75	42	10.00	420	1052	1.86
	100	29	14.00	406		
	150	6	25.00	150		
Total					56303.6	100

It is seen from the above table that Cinthol brand of toilet soap occupies the highest share of toilet soap market by value with 14.35%. The second and the third places are occupied by Lux brand and Beauty brand with 12.7% and 11.84% respectively. Though Beauty brand occupies the highest share by volume, yet it occupies third place in the share by value because of its lower MRP.

Market shares of toilet soap by size

Information presented in Table 12 is used for determining the market shares of toilet soap by size. Market shares of the different sizes of toilet soap by number of pieces consumed and by value are given in Table 13.

Table 13
Worksheet for the calculation of market shares of sizes of Toilet Soap

Size of Toilet Soap (gm.)	*No of pieces consumed*	*% Shares of sizes by no pieces*	*Total value of market of each sizes (Rs)*	*% Share of sizes by value*
50	57	1.30	279.5	0.49
70	7	0.16	56	0.09
75	2088	47.87	25438.1	45.18
80	297	6.81	2922	5.18
90	123	2.82	1107	1.96
100	1662	38.11	24188.5	42.96
125	52	1.19	674	1.19
150	75	1.71	1638.5	2.91
Total	4361	100	56303.6	100

It is evident from the above table that the size 75 gm occupies the highest share of market by pieces of consumption of toilet soap with 47.87% as well as the highest share of market by value with 45.18%. This is followed by 100 gm size of toilet soap with 38.11% share by pieces of consumption and 42.96% share by value of the toilet soap market.

Market shares of Toilet Soap by price range

Information given in Table 1 and Table 10 and Table 12 are used for the determination of market shares of toilet soaps by price ranges. Market shares of different price range of toilet soap by number of pieces consumed and by value are given in Table 14.

Table 14
Worksheet for the calculation of market share of toilet soap by price ranges of Toilet Soap

Price range of toilet soap	*No. of pieces consumed*	*% share sizesby no pieces*	*Total value of market of each sizes (Rs.)*	*% share of price ranges by value*
Less than Rs8/-	691	15.84	4668.5	8.29
Rs8/- but less than Rs12/-	2072	47.51	21610.6	38.38
Rs12/- but less than Rs16/-	878	20.13	12835.5	22.79
Rs16/- but less than Rs20/-	515	11.80	8788	15.68
Rs25/-	6	0.13	150	0.26
Rs29/-	44	1.00	1276	2.26
Rs45/-	155	3.55	6975	12.38
Total	4361	100	56303.6	100

It is observed from the above table that the maximum number of pieces of toilet soap is consumed by the households of Manipur at the price range of "Rs. 8/- but less than Rs.12/-" and this constitute 47.51 % of the pieces of toilet soap consumed. Further, this particular price range has the maximum share of the value of toilet soap market with 38.38%.

8. Household's and individual consumer's monthly average pieces of consumption, volume of consumption and monthly average expenditure on toilet soap

It is seen from the Table.4 that the total number of persons is 4500 in 752 households covered for the study. It is also found from Table.8 that the monthly total number of pieces of toilet soap consumed by these 752 households is 4361. As depicted by the Table.11, the total volume in grams consumed by these 752 households is 378720. Further, Table 12 presents that total expenditure or value of the toilet soap consumed by these 752 households is 56303.60 rupees. Information described above is used for the determination of the various values per household and per individual consumer as given in the following Table 15.

Table 15
Household's and individual consumer's monthly average pieces of consumption, volume of consumption of toilet soap and monthly average expenditure on Toilet Soap

Aspects	*Total consumption of sample households (a)*	*Average per household (a ÷ b)*	*Average per individual consumer (a ÷c)*
No of pieces	4361	5.79 (6 approx)	0.96 (1 approx)
Volume (gm.)	378720	503.61	84.16
Expenditure (value) inrupees	56303.6	74.87	12.51

Notes: 1. Total number of sampled households (b) =752
2. No of persons (c) in the 752 households = 4500

It is seen from the above table that the average pieces of toilet soap consumed per household and per individual consumer are 5.79 pieces (6 approx) and 0.96 pieces (1 approx) respectively. The volume of consumption per household is 503.61 gm. and the volume of consumption per individual consumer is 84.16 gm. Further, household's monthly expenditure on toilet soap is Rs. 74.87 and individual consumer's monthly expenditure on toilet soap is Rs. 12.51.

9. Estimated monthly total consumption of toilet soap and monthly total expenditure on toilet soap in Manipur

Information given in Table 15 regarding individual consumer's monthly average pieces of consumption, volume of consumption of toilet soap and monthly average expenditure on toilet soap is used for the various estimates given in the Table 16.

Table 16

Estimated monthly total consumption of Toilet Soap (pieces or volume) and monthly total expenditure (value) on Toilet Soap in Manipur

Parameters	*Districts*									
	Bishnupur	*Thoubal*	*Imphal East*	*Imphal West*	*Church-andpur*	*Senapati*	*Tameng-long*	*Ukhrul*	*Chandel*	*Manipur*
1	*2*	*3*	*4*	*5*	*6*	*7*	*8*	*9*	*10*	*11*
a. Population as per census 2001	205907	366341	393780	439532	228707	379214	111493	140946	122714	2388634
b. Monthly av. pieces of consumption of a Consumer	0.969	0.969	0.969	0.969	0.969	0.969	0.969	0.969	0.969	0.969
c. monthly av. volume (gm.) of consumption of a Consumer	84.16	84.16	84.16	84.16	84.16	84.16	84.16	84.16	84.16	84.16
d. Monthly av. expenditure on toilet soap by a consumer (Rs.)	12.51	12.51	12.51	12.51	12.51	12.51	12.51	12.51	12.51	12.51

(Contd....)

1	2	3	4	5	6	7	8	9	10	11
e. Estimated monthly consumption of toilet soap in pieces (a × b)	199523.88	354984.43	381572.82	425906.51	221617.08	367458.37	108036.72	136576.67	118909.87	2314586.3
f. Estimated monthly volume of toilet soap consumption (a ×c) gm.	17329133	30831259	33140525	36991013	19247981	31914650	9383250.9	11862015	10327610	201027000
g. Monthly av. Value of toilet market (a× d) (in Rupees)	2575896.6	4582925.9	4926187.8	5498545.3	2861124.6	4743967.1	1394777 .4	1763234.5	1535152.1	29881811

It is evident from the above table that the monthly estimated total number of pieces of toilet soap consumption in Manipur is 23,14,586. It also observed that the monthly estimated volume of consumption in Manipur is 201,027,000 gm. or 201.027 tones. Further, monthly estimated expenditure on toilet soap by the consumers of Manipur or the monthly value of toilet soap market in Manipur is Rs. 2,98,81,811 or Rs. 2.9881811 (crores).

It is also seen from the above table that Imphal West district has the highest value of toilet soap market among the districts of Manipur because of its largest population.

10. Per capita consumption of toilet soap in Manipur and in all India. Share of Manipur toilet soap market by volume in the Indian domestic market in the year 2001

For the purpose of determining the share of Manipur toilet soap market by volume in the Indian domestic market in the year 2001, the past trend and the projection of the purchase of toilet soap in India are given in Table 17 and Table 18 respectively.

Table 17
Year-wise purchase of toilet soap in India (past trend)

Year	*Volume (in tones)*
1985-86	227
1986-87	241
1987-88	289
1989-90	327
1992-93	433.51
1993-94	485.44

Source: S.L. Rio and I. Nataranjan; *Indian Market Demographic; The Consumer Class*; Global Business Press, National Council for Applied Economic Research - p. 183, 1996 edition.

Due to the non-availability of the current data, information given in the above table is used for the projection of toilet soap purchase for the year 2001. Detail Time Series Analysis for estimating the purchase of toilet soap in India is given in the *Appendix-I.* The projected figures are presented in the table given below.

Table 18
Projected year-wise purchase of toilet soap in India

Year	*Volume (000) tones*
1993	472.01
1994	503.9
1995	535.79
1996	567.68
1997	599.57
1998	631.46
1999	663.35
2000	695.24
2001	727.13

From the above table it is seen that the estimated total volume of consumption of toilet soap in India in the year 2001 is 727130 tonnes or 727130000 kg. And the population of India as per the 2001 census is 1,02,70,15,247 persons. Therefore, the per capita consumption of toilet soap in India is 0.70 kg (total consumption ÷total population).

From Table.15 it is evident that the estimated monthly average consumption of toilet soap per person in Manipur is 84.16 grams. Therefore the per capita consumption is 1009.92 grams (84.16 x 12) or 1.009 kg.

Information described above is presented in the following table.

Table 19
Per capita consumption of toilet soap in Manipur and in all India

Manipur	*All India*
1.009 kg	0.70 kg.

It is clear from the above table that the per capita consumption of toilet soap in Manipur is higher than that of all India. To be precise, per capita consumption of toilet soap in Manipur is 44.14% higher than that of all India.

Further, from the Table 16 the estimated monthly volume of toilet soap consumption in Manipur in the year 2001 is 201.027 tonnes. Thus, the estimated total consumption of toilet soap in the year 2001 is 2412.324 tonnes.

From the above information, share of Manipur toilet soap market by volume in the Indian domestic market in the year 2001 is presented in the Table 20.

Table 20
Estimated share of Manipur toilet soap market by volume in the Indian domestic market in the year 2001

Estimated consumption of toilet soap in the year 2001		
Manipur (000) tones	*All India (000) tones*	*% share of Manipur*
2.412324	727.13	0.33

It is evident from the above table that the share of the Manipur toilet soap market is 0.33% by volume in the Indian domestic market.

11. Share of Manipur toilet soap market by value in the Indian domestic market in the year 2001

Information regarding the past trend of domestic

consumption value of the toilet soap in India is used for the projection of the consumption value of toilet soap for the year 2001.

Table 21
Year-wise domestic consumption value of toilet soap (past trend)

Year	*Value in Crores*
1992-93	3985.5
1993-94	4355.1
1994-95	4644.3
1995-96	6248.3
1996-97	6758.7
1997-98	7477.4

Source: Centre of Monitoring Indian Economy; *Industry, Market Size and share,* p., 233, August, 1999 publication.

Due to non-availability of the updated data for the year 2001, information presented in the Table 21 is used for the estimation of the domestic consumption value of toilet soap for the year 2001.

Detail Time Series Analysis for projecting the domestic consumption value of toilet soap is given in the Appendix-II. The estimated year-wise value of consumption of toilet soap in India is furnished in the Table 22.

Table 22
Projected year-wise domestic consumption value of toilet soap in India

Year	*Value in Crores*
1997	7454.94
1998	8205.63
1999	8956.32
2000	9707.01
2001	10457.7

From Table 16, it is seen that the estimated monthly average value of toilet soap market in Manipur for the year 2001 is Rs. 2.9881811 crores. Therefore, the consumption value for the entire year 2001 is Rs. 35.8581732 crores.

With the help of the information described above, the share of Manipur toilet soap market by value in Indian domestic market is determined and presented in the table below.

Table 23

Estimated share of Manipur toilet soap market by value in the Indian domestic market in the year 2001

Estimated consumption value of toilet soap in the year 2001 (In Crores)		
Manipur	*All India*	*% share of Manipur*
35.8581732	10457.7	0.34

It is evident from the above table that Manipur consumer market of toilet soap occupies 0.34% share of the Indian domestic consumption value of toilet soap in the year 2001.

Consumer Market of Durable Goods (TV sets)

Tangible goods that normally survive many uses are known as durable goods. Examples include TV, refrigerator, washing machine etc.

TV receiver or TV set has become an essential household item for watching entertainment programs, educational programs, news etc. It is important for the marketers of TV to understand the characteristics of market so that they can formulate appropriate marketing strategies for the satisfaction of consumer needs and wants.

For having an idea about the consumer market of Manipur with special reference to durable goods (TV), the following aspects are discussed in this part of the chapter.

i) Households presently owning TV set(s).

ii) Households owning a single TV set or more.

iii) Preferred brands of TV by the households who do not presently own TV set.

iv) Brand-wise shares of TV set of the penetrated market.

v) Size-wise shares of TV sets of the penetrated market.

vi) Annual average growth rate of TV sets purchase.

vii) Annual average growth rate of value of TV sets purchased.

viii) Important marketers of TV whose products are presently available in Manipur.

ix) Sales of TV sets and market shares of different brands, sizes and price ranges by value in Manipur in the year 2001.

x) Share of TV sets sold in Manipur in the Indian domestic market of TV in the year 2001.

xi) Share of Manipur TV market by value in the Indian domestic market in the year 2001.

1. Households presently owning a TV set (till March 2002)

Depending upon the socio-economic background and the life-style, some households own TV set and some do not. In order to have an idea about the number of households owning TV set in Manipur, a total of 752 households consisting of 173, 151, 151, 179 and 98 households from *Bishnupur, Thoubal, Imphal East, Imphal West and Churchandpur districts* respectively were covered for the present study. Information in this aspect is presented in the following table.

Table 24
No. of households presently owning a TV set (till March 2002)

	No of Households – District-wise					
Status of Households	*Bishnupur*	*Thoubal*	*Imphal East*	*Imphal West*	*Churchand-pur*	*Total*
a. Owning	162	119	121	148	53	603
b. Not owning	11	32	30	31	45	149
Total	173	151	151	179	98	752
% of households owning TV	93.64	78.80	80.13	82.68	54.08	

It is evident from the above table that Bishnupur district has the highest number of TV ownership with 93.64%. The average percentage of TV ownership in the valley districts of Manipur i.e. Bishnupur, Thoubal, Imphal West, Imphal East

$$= \frac{162 + 119 + 121 + 148}{173 + 151 + 151 + 179} \text{x}100 = (550/654) \text{ x } 100 = 84.09\%$$

And the percentage of TV ownership in the hill district Churchandpur is 54.08%. This average figure has been considered for this study the overall average for the entire hill districts of Manipur.

The estimated number of households owning TV sets in Manipur is presented in the Table 25.

It is seen from the table 25 that out of the estimated total 3, 99,437 households of Manipur, 2, 86,552 households have owned TV set till March, 2002. The estimated percentage of TV owner in Manipur is 71.73%.

2. Households owning a single TV set or more

There is an increasing tendency to have multiple TV sets. This phenomenon is all the more significant with the increasing tendency of giving a TV set in every marriage as a gift in Manipur. An attempt is being made to determine the number of households owning a single TV set, two TV

Table 25

Estimated number of households owning TV set in Manipur

Population (2001) Census)			*Estimated no of households in*		*Households owning TV in*				
Valley districts (a)	*Hill districts (b)*	*Avg. Family size (Table 4) (c)*	*Valley districts (d)=a÷ c*	*Hill districts (e)=b÷ c*	*Valley districts (f)=84.09% (d)*	*Hill districts (g) =54.08% (d)*	*Total no of households inManipur owning TV(h) = (f + g)*	*Total no of households inManipur (i) = (d + e)*	*% of households owning TV in Manipur (f + g)÷ (d + e)*
1405560	983074	5.98 (6 approx)	235043	164394	197648	88904	286552	399437	71.73

Table 26
Households owning a single TV set, two TV sets, and three TV sets

No of TV		*No of Households – District-wise*								
		Bishnupur	*Thoubal*	*Imphal East*	*Imphal West*	*Churchandpur*	*Total*	*%*	*Total Category*	*%*
Single	Black & White	33	38	12	11	1	95	15.75	472	78.27
	Colour	85	63	87	93	49	377	62.52		
Two	B/B	1					1	0.16	122	20.23
	B/C	22	12	15	12	1	62	10.28		
	C/C	18	6	6	27	2	59	9.78		
Three	B/C/C	3		1	2		6	0.99	9	1.49
	C/C/C				3		3	0.49		
	Total	162	119	121	148	53	603	100	603	100

sets and three TV sets. Information in this aspect is presented in the Table 26.

It is seen from the Table 26 that 78.27% of the owners have a TV set each whereas 20.23% and 1.49% of the owners have two TV sets and three TV sets respectively.

Further, the table also reveals that 62.52% of TV owners have a single colour TV set whereas 15.75% of the owners have a single black and white TV sets. And 10.28% of the owners have two TV sets of which one is B& Wand the other is colour. It can also be inferred from the above table that in all there are 575 colour TV sets and 165 B&W TV sets.

3. Preferred brands of TV by the households who do not presently own TV

Information presented in Table 23 reveals that there are *149* households out of 752 sample households who do not own a TV set. Information gathered from them about the brand which they would like to buy in future is presented in the table given below.

Table 27
Preferred brands of TV by the households who do not presently own TV

Name of Brand/No Response	*No of Respondents - Districtwise*						
	Bishnupur	*Thoubal*	*Imphal East*	*Imphal West*	*Church-andpur*	*Total*	*%*
a. Philips	1	9	2	5	5	22	14.76
b. Sony	4	9	6	8	6	33	22.14
c. Onida		3	2	3	5	13	8.72
d. Videocon	1	6	1			8	5.36
e. Akai	1			1	3	5	3.35
f. L.G.		1	1	2		4	2.68
g. Sansui			1		2	3	2.01
h. BPL			2	2	2	6	4.02
i. AIWA			1	4		5	3.35
j. Manitron				1		1	0.67
k. Samsung					3	3	2.01
l. No response	4	4	14	5	19	46	30.87
Total	11	32	30	31	45	149	100

It is observed from the above table that Sony occupies the highest brand share among the brands that people who do not presently own a TV set would like to purchase in future. Sony accounts for 22.14% followed by Philips and Onida brands with 14.70% and 8.72% respectively. It is also seen that 30% of the respondents who presently do not own a TV set have not given any response.

4. Brand-wise share of TV sets of the penetrated market

It is already known from the preceding portions of the present chapter that 603 households out of 752, own TV set and some owners have a single TV set and some, more than one TV set. It is also seen that the total no of TV sets in the 603 households is 740, consisting of 575 colour and 165 black and white.

In order to determine the market share of brands separately for colour and B& W, brand wise no of pieces of TV set penetrated district-wise are presented in the following Table.28 and Table.29.

Brand-wise share of TV in Colour Segment:

Table 28
Brand-wise share of TV sets of the penetrated market in the Colour Segment

Brand Name	*No of pieces of TV Sets - District-wise*						
	Bishnupur	*Thoubal East*	*Imphal West*	*Imphal andpur*	*Church-*	*Total*	*%*
1	*2*	*3*	*4*	*5*	*6*	*7*	*8*
1. Onida	19	15	16	26	11	87	15.13
2. Sony	24	12	7	22	16	81	14.08
3. Philips	17	9	5	24	6	61	10.60
4. Videocon	22	17	17	18	2	76	13.21

(Contd....)

1	*2*	*3*	*4*	*5*	*6*	*7*	*8*
5. Manitron	23	3	12	12	5	55	9.56
6. L.G.	6	1	17	11	5	40	6.95
7. Aiwa	11	7	9	7	2	36	6.26
8. BPL	6	3	9	8	1	27	4.69
9. Akai	5	1	8	14		28	4.86
10. Thomson		2	8	2	2	14	2.43
11. Sansui	2	6	1	2		11	1.91
12. Beltex	4		1			5	0.86
13. Weston	1	4		2		7	1.21
14. Sangai	1		5	1		7	1.21
15. T -Series	1	1				2	0.34
16. Oscar	1	1	1			3	0.52
17. Samsung	1			2	2	5	0.86
18. Nelco	1			2		3	0.52
19. Telerama	1			3		4	0.69
20. Bush	1	2				3	0.52
21. Konka		1		2		3	0.52
22. Orson				2		2	0.34
23. Televista				2		2	0.34
24. Dynora				1	1	2	0.34
25. Others	2	2		6	1	11	1.91
Total	149	87	116	169	54	575	100.00

Note: Others include 11 brands. They are Texla, Salora, Tulsi, TCL, Binaton, Panasonic, Vistavision, Kono, Hitachi and Goldstar.

It is observed from the above table that Onida brand has the highest share of penetrated market in the colour segment with 15.13% of TV sets followed by Sony brand in the second place with 14.08%. And the third place goes to by Videocon brand with 13.21 %.

Brand-wise share of TV in black & white segment

Table 29
Brand-wise share of TV sets of the penetrated market in Black & White segment

	Brand Name	*No of pieces of TV Sets - District-wise*						
		Bishnupur	*Thoubal*	*Imphal East*	*Imphal West*	*Churchandpur*	*Total*	*%*
1.	Onida	13	13	3	3		32	19.39
2.	Sony	1	2				3	1.81
3.	Philips	9	10	9	3		31	18.78
4.	Video con	4	4	3	1		12	7.27
5.	Manitron	5	1	4	5		15	9.09
6.	BPL		1	3			4	2.42
7.	Beltex	7	3	4	3		17	10.30
8.	Weston		6				6	3.63
9.	Sangai	1		1			2	1.21
10.	T-Series	1	3				4	2.42
11.	Salora	3	2			1	6	3.63
12.	Telerama	4		1			5	3.03
13.	Bush	1	1		1		3	1.81
14.	Texla	2					2	1.21
15.	DTV	2					2	1.21
16.	Etxt	2					2	1.21
17.	DYNORA		1			1	2	1.21
18.	Uptron		2				2	1.21
19.	Oscar				2		2	1.21
20.	Nelco				3		3	1.81
21.	Others	5	1		4		10	6.06
	Total	60	50	28	25	2	165	100

Note: Others include 10 brands. They are Orson, Keltron, Cathy, Hagalin, Televista, Supertron, Panasonic, Canon, Star and Citizen.

The above table depicts that Onida brand of TV has the highest share in the penetrated market which accounts for 19.39%. In the second place Philips brand accounts for 18.78% and third place is occupied by Beltex brand with 10.30% of TV sets.

5. Size-wise share of TV sets of the penetrated market

In case of colour TV the most popular size is 21 inch model which accounts for 84.52% of the penetrated market. The second place is occupied by the size of 14 inch accounting for 7.65%.

But in the case of black and white TV segment the most popular size is 14 inch, which accounts for 84.24% and the second place is occupied by size 21 inch with 13.93% of Black and White segment. The above description is based on the information presented in the Table 30.

6. Annual average growth rate of TV set purchase

It was only in the year 1982, when IX Asian games were held in Delhi, TV signal reached Manipur for telecasting the game.

Since then, people of Manipur started purchasing TV set. It is 603 households of the 752 sample households which have owned TV set till March 2002. In these 603 households there are 575 colour and 165 black and white TV sets. The average annual growth rate of TV set purchase in these households will be similar to that of Manipur because of the use of area sampling method for the purpose of the present study.

Annual average growth rate of colour TV sets purchase

Year-wise purchase of colour TV by the sample households is presented in the following table for the determination of the average annual growth rate of colour TV.

Table 30
Size-wise share of TV sets of the penetrated market

Size (in inch)	Bishnupur			Thoubal			Imphal East			Impal West			Churchandpur			Total				Over all Total	% Share of Size
	Color	B & W	Total	Color	B & W	Total	Color	B & W	Total	Color	B & W	Total	Color	B & W	Total	color	%	B & W	%		
14	8	50	58	4	44	48	14	22	36	15	23	38	3		3	44	7.65	139	84.24	183	24.72
20	1		1	1		1	6	2	8	10	1	11	1		1	19	3.30	3	1.81	22	2.97
21	139	10	149	82	6	88	88	4	92	140	1	141	37	2	39	486	84.52	23	13.93	509	68.78
22	1		1				8		8	4		4	13		13	26	4.52			26	3.51
Total	149	60	209	87	50	137	116	28	144	169	25	194	54	2	56	575	100	165	100	740	100

Table 31
Annual average growth rate of colour TV sets purchase

Year	*No. of TV sets purchase – district-wise*							
	Bishnupur	*Thoubal*	*Imphal East*	*Imphal West*	*Churchandpur*	*Total*	*Annual Growth Rate*	*Av. Annual Growth Rate*
1	*2*	*3*	*4*	*5*	*6*	*7*	*8*	*9*
1982	4		1	2		7	——	
1983				2		2	-71.42	
1984	1	1		1		3	50.00	
1985		2		1	1	4	33.33	
1986	1	1	1	2		5	25.00	
1987		1	4	1		6	20.00	
1988				1		1	-83.33	
1989		2	4	1	2	9	8000.00	
1990	3	3	5	2	1	14	55.55	
1991	2	1				3	-78.57	
1992	1	5	4	4	1	15	400	=1377.3/19
1993	7	2		4		13	-13.33	=72.48%
1994	8	1	6	5	2	22	96.23	

(Contd....)

1	*2*	*3*	*4*	*5*	*6*	*7*	*8*	*9*
1995	13	5	6	16	1	41	86.36	
1996	4	6	5	13	1	29	-29.26	
1997	15	5	10	12	2	44	51.72	
1998	24	12	13	27	7	83	88.63	
1999	24	10	11	23	6	74	-10.84	
2000	11	15	23	26	12	87	17.52	
2001	14	10	10	18	6	58	-33.33	
2002	17	5	13	8	12	55		
Total	149	87	116	169	54	575	1377.3	

Note: Data for the year 2002 are up to month of March only. So, data for this year are not included for the calculation of the average annual growth rate.

It is evident from the Table 31 that the average annual growth rate of colour TV set purchased in Manipur is 72.48% during the period 1982-2001. A deep look into the annual growth rate reveals that there are two extreme annual growth rates of 800% in the year 1989 and 400% in 1992 and two extreme negative growth rate of 83.33% and 78.57% in the year1988 and 1991 respectively. If these four extremes are discarded, the representation growth rate during the period 1982-2001 is 22.61%. Further, average growth rate during the period 1995-2001 is 14.08%. (i.e., (-29.26 + 51.72 + 88.63 - 10.84 + 17.56- 33.33) / 6

Annual average growth rate of Black and White TV purchase

Year-wise purchase of B& W TV by the sample households is given in the Table 32 for determining the average annual growth rate of B& W TV.

It is clear from the Table 32 that average annual growth rate of the purchase of B& W TV is 16.58%. Further, it also reveals that the annual growth rate during the period 1995-2001 is - 13.76% (i.e. 0 - 35.71 + 0 - 22.22 + 57.14 -81.81)/6 In other words, purchase during this period is declining at the rate of 13.76% annually.

7. Annual average growth rate of value of TV sets purchase

Year-wise value of TV purchase is computed by taking the total of prices at which TV sets are purchased by consumers in a particular year.

Average growth rate of value of colour TV purchase

Year-wise value of colour TV purchased by the sample households Manipur is presented in the Table 33.

Table 32
Annual average growth rate of B& W TV sets purchase

Year	*No. of TV sets purchase – district-wise*							
	Bishnupur	*Thoubal*	*Imphal East*	*Imphal West*	*Churchand pur*	*Total*	*Annual Growth Rate*	*Av. Annual Growth Rate*
1	*2*	*3*	*4*	*5*	*6*	*7*	*8*	*9*
1982	4	1		2		7		
1983		1		1		2	-71.42	
1984	2	1	1	1		5	150	
1985	4	1	2	3		10	100	
1986	2	2		1		5	-50	
1987	4	1	5		1	11	120	
1988	2	2	1			5	-54.54	
1989	2	3	2	2		9	80	
1990	3	3	1	4		11	22.22	
1991	3	3	1			7	-36.36	

(Contd....)

1	2	3	*4*	*5*	*6*	*7*	*8*	*9*
1992	4	4	2	1		11	57.14	=315.17/19
1993	2	2	1	3		8	-27.27	=16.58
1994	3	3				6	-25.00	
1995	6	6	1	1		14	133	
1996	7	4	2	1		14		
1997	4	1	2	2		9	-35.71	
1998	4	4	1			9		
1999	2	1	1	2	1	7	-22.22	
2000	2	5	3	1		11	57.14	
2001		1	1			2	-81.81	
2002		1	1			2		
Total	60	50	28	25	2	165	315.17	

Note: Data for the year 2002 are up to month of March only. So, data for this year are not included for the calculation of the average annual growth rate.

Table 33

Annual average growth rate market value of colour TV purchase

Year	No. of TV sets purchase – district-wise							
	Bishnupur	Thoubal	Imphal East	Imphal West	Churchandpur	Total	Annual Growth Rate	Av. Annual Growth Rate
1	2	3	4	5	6	7	8	9
1982	69		21	45		135	—	
1983				33		33	-75.55	
1984	21	19		12		52	57.57	
1985		40.4		19	22.5	81.9	57.50	
1986	17	11.5	17	26		71.5	-12.69	
1987		13	59	14		86	20.27	
1988				17		17	-80.23	
1989		26	63	13	32	134	688.23	
1990	46	59	77.65	23.5	11	217.15	62.05	
1991	32.5	18				50.5	-76.74	

(Contd....)

1	2	3	4	5	6	7	8	9
1992	18	75.3	55	63	22	233.3	361.98	=1236.89/19
1993	104.1	28.5		50		182.6	-21.73	=65.5
1994	132.5	12.5	99	73	41	358	96.05	
1995	211.35	17.1	75	241.5	14	612.95	71.21	
1996	75	95	75	193.1	18	456.1	-25.58	
1997	247.7	84.5	151	190.5	44.5	718.2	57.46	
1998	411.3	180.57	212.1	385.2	112.7	1301.87	81.26	
1999	412.549	163.8	156.639	442	102.6	1277.588	-1.86	
2000	179	237.2	360.199	392.5	224.5	1393.399	9.06	
2001	260.29	132.099	136.51	307.5	119	955.399	-31.43	
2002	293.57	68.8	207	127.5	200.9	897.82		
Total							1236.89	

Note: Data for the year 2002 are up to month of March only. So, data for this year are not included for the calculation of the average annual growth rate.

The Table 33 depicts that the average annual growth rate of value of colour TV purchase in Manipur is 65.05% during the period 1982-2001. Further, analysis reveals that there are two extreme annual growth rate of 688.23% and 361.98% in the year 1989 and 1992 and two extreme negative growth rates of 80.23% and 76.74% in the year 1988 and 1991 respectively. If these four extremes are discarded, the representative annual growth rate is 22.91 %. Moreover, the annual average growth rate during the period 1995-2001 is 14.87%. {i.e. (-25.58 + 57.46 + 81.26 - 1.86 + 9.06 - 31.43) / 6}

Annual average growth rate of value of B&W TV Purchase

Year-wise value of B& W TV purchased by the sample households is presented in the Table 34 for evaluating the average annual growth rate of value of B&W TV purchase.

It is seen from the Table 34 that the average annual growth rate of value of B&W TV purchase in Manipur is 16.57% during the period 1982-2001. Further, it reveals that the average growth rate of B& W TV purchase during the period 1995-2001 is (-) 20.93% { i.e. (-23.38 + 33.78 + 12.17 + 23.27 - 82.71) / 6 }. In other words, market value of the B& W TV in Manipur is declining in the recent years at the rate of 20.93% annually.

8. Important marketers of TV whose products are presently available in Manipur

It is seen from the above table that in all there are 9 brands of TV which are presently available in the Manipur market with various size and price ranges. Flat TV models have recently entered into Manipur TV market.

9. Sales of TV sets and market share of brands, sizes and price ranges by value in Manipur in the year 2001

In Manipur, there are 7 main dealers of TV marketing

Table 34
Annual average growth rate of value of B&W TV purchase

Year	No. of TV sets purchase – district-wise							
	Bishnupur	Thoubal	Imphal East	Imphal West	Churchand-pur	Total	Annual Growth Rate	Av. Annual Growth Rate
1	2	3	4	5	6	7	8	9
1982	21	3.5		7		31.5		
1983		4		5		9	-71.42	
1984	6.1	3.5	5	4		18.6	106.66	
1985	22.9	5	10	13		50.9	173.65	
1986	12.5	11.5		4		28	-44.99	
1987	17.5	4	18.8		6	46.35	65.53	
1988	7	8.8	3.5			19..3	-58.36	
1989	10.5	15.4	10	12		47.9	148.18	
1990	20	11.3	3.5	17		51.8	8.14	
1991	13	11.2	10			30.2	-41.69	

(Contd....)

1	*2*	*3*	*4*	*5*	*6*	*7*	*8*	*9*
1992	29	16.588	3.5	4		55.088	82.41	=314.94/19
1993	8	8.1	6	11.5		30.6	-44.45	=16.57
1994	14.8	17.25	5.5			32.05	4.73	
1995	33.5	26.5	3	4		68	112.16	
1996	25.1	16.5		7		52.1	-23.38	
1997	12.5	5	4	7		34.5	-33.78	
1998	19.2	16.5	3.5			38.7	12.17	
1999	9	3.5	10	7.5	7	30.5	-21.18	
2000	5.7	16.5	12.1	3.5		37.6	23.27	
2001		3	3.5			6.5	-82.71	
2002		2.5	2.5			5.5		
Total							314.94	

Note: Data for the year 2002 are up to month of March only. So, data for this year are not included for the calculation of the average annual growth rate.

Table 35

Important marketers of TV whose products are presently available in Manipur and their brands, varieties, sizes and MRPs

				Types					
Sl. No.	*Name of the company*	*Brand name*	*Variety*	*B&W*		*Colour*		*Flat screen*	
				Size (inch)	*MRP (Rs)*	*Size (inch)*	*MRP (Rs)*	*Size(inch)*	*MRP (Rs)*
	1	*2*	*3*	*4*	*5*	*6*	*7*	*8*	*9*
1.	L.G.	L.G.	Cine plus			14	7990		
			Cine plus gold			20	10690		
			Golden Eye Magic			20	11490		
			Soccer TV			20	13990		
			Sound Master			20	12990		
			Supreme			20	14990		
			Supreme			20	18600		
			Flatron			21	21200		
			Flatron Gold					21	16990
			Flatron Gold					21	23000
								21	25000
			Golden Eye (Marquis)			29	24990		
			Golden Eye (Woofer)			29	26990		
			Golden Eye (Woofer+PIP)				29	28990	

(Contd....)

	1	*2*	*3*	*4*	*5*	*6*	*7*	*8*	*9*
2.	Videocon	Videocon	Snazz			21	11990		
			Bazzon			21	16990		
			Bazoomba			21	16990		
			Bazoomba			25	17990		
3.	Philips	Philips	Digicolour			20	9990		
			Zappa			20	10990		
			Digicolour			21	14990		
			Digicolour			21	12490		
			Digicolour Flat					21	23490
	Philips	Philips	Digicolour (B&W)	14	2644				
			-do-	17	3025				
			-do-	17	4085				
4.	Onida	Onida	Candy			14	8990		
			-do-			20	12490		
			21 TVE Small Series			21	13990		
			20 TVE (-do-)			20	10990		
			KY Thunder			21	17990		
			Kyrock			21	14990		
			Audioport			21	14990		
			Multiview (PIP)			21	19990		
			Black					21	15990
			Black(Bass Blaster)					21	18990

(Contd....)

	1	2	3	4	5	6	7	8	9
5.	Thomson	Thomson	Color track			14	7990		
			Life line			14	9990		
			Corda			20	10990		
			Fusion			21	12990		
			Slime line			21	13490		
			White pearl			21	17990		
			Black diva			25	24990		
			Fusion			29	26990		
			Color track			29	29990		
6.	Sony	Sony	B-14			14	12490		
			HA14M80 (WEGA)					14	15990
			J21			21	17990		
	Sony	Sony	HA21M80(WEGAI)					21	18990
			XF21 M80(WEGA)					21	19990
			XA21N83 (WEGA)					21	23100
			XA21N93 (WEGA)					21	25200
			XA25M80 (WEGA)					25	34990
			XJ29M80 (WEGA)					29	49990
			XA29M97 (WEGA)					29	52990
			XA34M97(WEGA)					34	52990
			EX34M97(WEGA-ORC)					34	109000
	Sony	Sony	XA34M97 (WEGA)					34	84990
			XA29M80 (WEGA)					29	44990

(Contd....)

	1	2	3	4	5	6	7	8	9
7.	Samsung	Samsung	14E4			14	6990		
			2004			20	10200		
			2008			20	11500		
			21E4			21	12590		
			2108			21	16490		
			1408			14	9600		
			PLANO						
			21K5					21	18000
			21T3					21	23990
			29M6					29	49990
			25M6					25	30990
8.	BPL	BPL	ATR			14	6990		
			PRIMA			20	9900		
			PRIMA			21	10990		
	BPL	BPL	FER					21	20000
			FSR					21	24500
9.	Akai	Akai	CT2020			20	10500		
			CT2126			21	11000		
			CT2222(Power Flat)					21	18500
			CT2121D (Black Belt)			21	14000		
			CT1403 (Black belt model)			14	9500		

Note: Manipur Electronics Development Corporation Limited (MANITRON), a Govt. of Manipur Undertaking which assembles and markets Manitron brand of TV is not included in the above list because the corporation is not doing any business activities for the last one year.

Philips and Onida, Thomson and Sony, LG, Samsung, BPL and Akai brands of TV respectively.

Information regarding monthly average sales (approx) of each size of TV sets was gathered from them and presented in the following table for assessing total value of sales, brand-wise share of value and size wise share of value for the year 2001.

Brand-wise share of value of TV sets sold in the year 2001

Table 36
Brand wise share of market value of TV sets sold in 2001

Brand name	*Size*	*No. of pieces sold per month*	*MRP/Av. MRP of the same size (Rs.)*	*Size wise value (000) (Rs)*	*Brand wise value (000) (Rs.)*	*% share of brand*
1	*2*	*3*	*4*	*5*	*6*	*7*
1.L.G	14	150	7990	1198.5		
	20	20	13791	275.82		
	21	50	21200	1060.00		
					3055.783	30.45
	29	20	24990	499.80		
Flat	21	1	21663	21.663		
2. Videocon	21	50	15323	766.15		
					1305.85	13.01
	25	30	17990	539.7		
3. Philips	20	5	10490	52.45		
	21	5	13740	68.7		
Flat	21	1	23490	23.49	188.855	1.88
B&W	14	10	2644	26.44		
B&W	17	5	3555	17.775		
4. Onida	14	5	8990	44.95		
	20	5	11740	58.70	267.55	2.66
	21	10	16390	163.9		
5. Sony	14	5	12490	62.45		

(Contd....)

1	*2*	*3*	*4*	*5*	*6*	*7*
	21	10	17990	179.9	590.962	5.89
Flat	25	2	34990	69.98		
Flat	14	1	15990	15.99		
Flat	29	2	34326	68.652		
Flat	34	2	96995	193.99		
6. BPL	14	10	6990	69.9		
	20	10	9990	99.9	356.9	3.55
	21	15	10990	164.85		
Flat	21	1	22250	22.25		
7. Thomson	14	10	8990	89.9		
	20	5	10990	54.95		
	21	10	14823	148.23	458.02	4.56
	25	3	24990	74.97		
	29	3	29990	89.97		
8. Akai	21	100	12500	1250		
	20	80	10500	840	3130	31.19
	14	90	9500	855		
Flat	21	10	18500	185		
9. Samsung	14	5	8295	41.475		
	20	10	10850	108.5		
	21	25	14540	363.5	678.435	6.76
Flat	21	4	20995	83.98		
Flat	29	1	49990	49.99		
Flat	25	1	30990	30.990		
Total		782			10032.355	

Note: B& W TV is included in this table. Separate analysis is not done because of its low sales and non-availability of brands other than Philips.

It is evident from the above table that Akai brand has the highest market share of value accounting for 31.19%. It is followed by L.G and Videocon brands with 30.45% and 13.0% respectively.

It is also seen from the above table that the monthly sales of TV set in Manipur is approximately 782 pieces amounting to Rs 10032.355 thousands or Rs. 1.0032355 crores.

So the estimated number of TV sets sold and total value of the market in Manipur for the year 2001 is presented in the table given below.

Table 37
Estimated total sales of TV and market value of TV market in Manipur in the year 2001

Period	*TV sets sold (units)*	*Value of TV market (crores)*
Monthly average	782	1.0032355
For the year 2001 (avg.× 12)	9384	12.0388260

It is clear from the above table that approximate number of TV sets sold in Manipur in the year 2001 is 9384 pieces and the value of the market is Rs. 12.0338826 crores.

Size-wise share of market value of TV sets sold in the year 2001

Information given in the Table.36 is used for the determination of the size wise share of value of TV sold in Manipur in the year 2001. Size-wise pieces sold monthly and value of each size is presented in the Table given below.

Table 38
Size-wise share of value of TV sets sold in the year 2001

Sizes (inches)	*Pieces sold per Month*	*Values (000) Rs*	*% share of value*
14"	286	2404.605	23.96
17"	5	17.775	0.177
20"	135	1490.320	14.85
21"	292	4501.613	44.87
25"	36	715.64	7.13
29"	26	708.412	7.06
34"	2	193.99	1.93
Total	782	10032.355	100

It is clear from the above table that the size 21 inches has the highest market share of TV sold with 44.87%. This is followed by 14 inches size model with 23.96% and the third place is occupied by 20-inch size model with 14.85%. Price range-wise share of market value of TV sets sold in the year 2001. Information given in the Table 36 is used for assessing the price range wise share of value of TV sets sold in the year 2001. Price range wise pieces sold monthly and the values of each price range are presented in the following table.

Table 39
Price range-wise share of market value of TV sold in the year 2001

Price range	*No. of pieces sold per month*	*Value '000' Rs.*	*% share of value*
Below Rs. 10,000	295	2443.84	24.35
Rs. 10,000 but less than Rs. 15,000	285	3448.15	34.37
Rs. 15,000 but lessthan Rs. 20,000	111	1850.64	18.44
Rs. 20,000 but less than Rs. 25,000	80	1786.153	17.80
Rs. 25,000 and above	11	503.372	5.01
Total	782	10032.355	100

It is seen from the above table that the price range "Rs. 10,000 but less than Rs. 15,000" occupies the highest share which accounts for 34.37% of the market value. This is followed by the price range "below Rs. 10,000" with 24.5%.

Moreover, price range "Below Rs. 10,000" has the maximum number of units sold which is followed by the price range "Rs. 10,000 but less than Rs. 15,000".

10 Share of TV sets sold in Manipur in the Indian domestic market of TV in the year 2001

The past trend and the projection of the purchase of TV in the year Indian domestic market are presented in the following Table 40 and Table 41 respectively.

Table 40
Year-wise purchase of TV set in India (past trend)

Year	*No of units (in million) (both colour and black and white)*
1985-85	2
1986-87	2.8
1987-89	3.6
1989-90	5.2
1992-93	4.22
1993-94	5.18

Source: S.L. Rao and I. Nataranjan; *Indian Market demographic, the consumer class*; Global Business Press, National Council of Applied Economic Research; p. 169, 1996.

Due to inaccessibility of the updated data, information given in the above table is used in the projection of TV set purchase for the year 2001. Time series analysis for estimating the purchase of TV sets in Indian domestic market is given in the Appendix III. The estimated figures are given in the table below.

Table 41
Projected year-wise purchase of TV in India

Year	*No of units (in million) (both colour and black and white)*
1993	5.25
1994	5.577
1995	5.904
1996	6.231
1997	6.558
1998	6.885
1999	7.212
2000	7.539
2001	7.866

From the above table, it is evident that the estimated total purchase of TV set in India in the year 2001 is 7.866 millions units or 7866000 pieces of TV sets. This information and the information given in the Table 37 is used for ascertaining the share of TV sets sold in Manipur in the Indian domestic market in the year 2001.

Table 42
Estimated share of TV sets sold in Manipur in the Indian domestic market of TV in the year 2001

Estimated no of TV sets sold in		*% share of Manipur*
Manipur	All India	
9384	7866000	0.119

It is seen from the above table that the share of TV set purchase in Manipur in the year 2001 is 0.119% of the all India domestic market.

11. Share of Manipur TV market by value in the Indian domestic market in the year 2001

For examining the share of Manipur in the Indian domestic consumption value of TV, information regarding the past trend of domestic consumption value of TV sets is used for estimating the value of TV sets purchased in the year 2001. Information about the past trend is presented in the following table.

Table 43
Year-wise domestic consumption value TV receivers

Year	*Value in crores*
1992-93	2446.4
1993-94	2946.6
1994-95	2778.9
1995-96	3463.1
1996-97	4204.3
1997-98	5478.0

Source: Industry, market size and share, Centers for Monitoring Indian Economy, p. 233, August 1999 publications.

Due to the non-availability of the information for the year 2001, information given in the above table is used for the estimation of the domestic consumption value of TV receiver for all India for the year 2001. Detail time series analysis for estimating the domestic consumption value of TV receiver for the year 2001 is given in the Appendix - IV. The projected year-wise value of consumption is given in the following table.

Table 44
Projected year-wise domestic consumption value of TV sets in India

Year	*Value in crores*
1997	4953.95
1998	5514.38
1999	6074.81
2000	6635.24
2001	7195.67

It is observed from the above table that the estimated domestic consumption value of TV in India for the year 2001 is Rs. 7195.67 crores. This information and the information given in the Table 37 is used for the evaluation of share of the value of Manipur TV market in the Indian domestic market in the year 2001 as given below.

Table 45
Estimated share of Manipur TV market value in the Indian domestic market in the year 2001

Estimated Consumption Value of TV market (in crores)		*% share of Manipur*
In Manipur	All India	
12.038826	7195.67	0.167

It is evident from the above table that in Manipur consumer market of TV accounts for 0.167% in the Indian domestic consumption value in the year 2001.

4

Present Scenario of Consumer Buying Behaviour in Manipur

Introduction

Consumer buying behaviour which is referred to as the buying behaviour of the final consumers who buy goods and services for personal consumption entails what the consumers buy, why they buy it, how often they buy it and how often they use it.

Present chapter is an exercise in the direction to examine consumer buying behaviour in Manipur in respect of the products chosen for the study i.e., consumer non-durable goods (toilet soap) and consumer durable goods (TV). The description in this chapter has been made on the basis of primary data that have been collected through questionnaire served to 752 respondents (households) covering 5 districts of Manipur.

The information thus collected has been tabulated, analysed and presented in the following paragraphs.

This chapter has been divided into three parts. The first part presents the consumer's backgrounds, while the second part discusses the consumer buying behaviour of non-durable goods (toilet soap) and part three describes the consumer buying behaviour of durable goods (TV).

Consumer's Background

The consumer's background i.e. culture, personality and social class influences consumer's decisions. Different emphasis is given by different cultures, personalities and social classes in the buyer's choice of brand, purchase amount, purchase timing, dealer, etc. And attempt is made to determine the culture, the personality and the social class to which the consumers of Manipur belong to. This portion of the chapter presents the consumer's culture, personality and social class.

1. *Consumer's Culture*

The consumer behaviour that is the things they buy is influenced by consumer's background or culture. For the purpose of the present study, consumers of Manipur are assumed to be exposed to the cultures and values of achievement, positive, independent, materialistic, social or interactive and health or fitness. Appropriate statements corresponding to the above cultures are given in the questionnaire. The statements are:

a) I worry about what will happen if my plans do not work out.

b) I don't get disappointed when things do not go my way.

c) I enjoy working along.

d) I prefer to spend Sundays and holidays in doing works and earning rather than spending time with family and friends.

e) I take initiative in making friendship with people.

f) I wake up early in the morning for keeping in good health.

The respondents are asked to indicate the statement which suits to their opinion about themselves. The responses so collected are tabulated in the following Table 46.

Table 46
Consumer's culture

	No. of Respondents – District-wise						
Culture Category	*Bishnupur*	*Thoubal*	*Imphal East*	*Imphal West*	*Church-andpur*	*Total*	*Per-centage*
a. Achievement	42	21	27	32	34	156	20.74
b. Positive	15	16	36	28	28	123	16.35
c. Independent	18	17	37	30	13	115	15.29
d. Materialistic	36	15	14	11	11	87	11.56
e. Social or Interactive	25	32	20	29	2	108	14.36
f. Health or Fitness	37	50	17	49	10	163	21.67
Total	173	151	151	179	98	752	100

The above table speaks clearly that health or fitness occupies the first place as it is indicated by more number of respondents i.e. 163 out of 752 respondents (21.67%). Second and third places are occupied by achievement and positive cultures respectively with 20.74% and 16.35% of respondents. Further, the figures in the table reveal that achievement constitutes the highest share of culture within the districts of Bishnupur and Churchandpur, health or fitness within the districts of Imphal West and Thoubal and independent within Imphal East district.

2. *Consumer's personality*

Personality factor is a useful variable in analysing consumer behaviour. Marketers often try to develop brand images that match the target market's personality and self-image. Kerene Horney proposed that "individuals can be classified into three personality groups, namely compliant, aggressive and detache".[26] Compliant individuals desire to be loved, wanted and appreciated. Aggressive individuals desire to excel and win admiration. Detached individuals desire independence, self-reliant, self-sufficient and freedom from obligation. In this aspect three statements are served to the respondents in the questionnaire. The statements corresponding to Compliant, Aggressive and Detached personality are given below:

a) I always have a desire to be loved and appreciated.

b) I always have a desire to excel and win admiration.

c) I always have a desire to be independent, self-reliant and freedom from obligation.

The responses collected from the respondents are presented in the Table 47.

Table 47
Consumer's personality

	No. of Respondents – District Wise						
Personality Category	*Bishnupur*	*Thoubal*	*Imphal East*	*Imphal West*	*Church-andpur*	*Total*	*Per-centage*
a. Complaint	53	27	57	56	16	209	27.79
b. Aggressive	38	36	41	33	52	200	26.59
c. Detached	82	88	53	90	30	343	45.61
Total	173	151	151	179	98	752	100

It is evident from the above table that the majority of the respondents i.e. 45.61 % belong to the detached personality whereas 27.79% and 26.52% of 161 respondents belong to compliant and aggressive personality respectively. Further, it may be mentioned that within the districts of Bishnupur, Thoubal and Imphal West detached personality occupies the highest share whereas within the districts of Imphal East compliant personality occupies the highest share. And in the district Churchandpur Aggressive personality occupies the highest share.

3. *Consumer's Social Class*

Social class which refers to the group of people that share equal position in a society also plays very important role in influencing the consumers in their buying decision. Here, subjective measure is employed by serving a question to the respondents asking them to indicate the social class, which they belong to. The responses are computed in the following Table 48.

Table48
Consumer's social class

Social Class Category	*No. of Respondents – District-wise*					*Total*	*Per-centage*
	Bishnupur	*Thoubal*	*Imphal East*	*Imphal West*	*Church-andpur*		
a. Upper Class	7	3	19	21	2	52	6.91
b. Middle Class	145	135	107	133	65	585	77.79
c. Lower Class	21	13	25	25	31	115	15.29
Total	173	151	151	179	98	752	100.00

It may be seen from the table that majority of the respondents i.e. 77.79% belong to middle social class. This is followed by lower social class and upper social class with 15.29% and 6.91 % of respondents respectively. Further, the table also reveals that the middle class occupies highest share in all the districts.

Consumer Buying Behaviour of Non-durable Goods (Toilet Soap)

Non-durable goods are the tangible goods that normally are consumed in one or few uses. Toilet soap belongs to the non-durable goods category. Soap is a substance used with water for washing and cleaning. Soap is made of fat or oil combined with an alkali. And the toilet soap refers to the soap used for cleaning oneself. In today's modem society, toilet soap has become an important household item in everyone's day to day life. Consumer buying behaviour of toilet soap is being discussed in this part of the chapter. This portion covers the following aspects:

i) Consumer's awareness level of different brands

ii) Consumer's sources of information

iii) Product factors and marketing factors involved in the choice of a particular brand

iv) Buying roles

v) Purchase brands, outlets of purchase, and purchase amount

vi) Consumer's satisfaction with the brands presently in use

vii) Brand loyalty

viii) Types of buying behaviour.

1. *Consumer's awareness level of different brands of toilet soap*

Awareness plays very important role in the consumer's buying decision. Awareness is the first step in the adoption process i.e., awareness, interest, evaluation, trial and adoption. It is also the beginning of buyer's readiness states i.e., awareness, knowledge, liking, preference, conviction and purchase. Moreover, product trial rate is also related with the awareness level. In order to get an idea about the consumer's awareness level, information was collected in this aspect and presented in the following Table 49.

Table 49
Consumer's awareness level of different brands of Toilet Soap

Name of the Brands	*No. of Respondents – District-wise*						
	Bishnupur	*Thoubal*	*Imphal East*	*Imphal West*	*Churchandpur*	*Total*	*Percentage*
1. Cinthol	170	140	151	179	85	725	96.4
2. Lux	173	151	151	179	98	752	100
3. Beauty	130	115	120	100	91	556	73.93
4. Lifebouy	173	151	151	179	83	737	98
5. Liril	120	115	105	150	71	561	74.60
6. Nirma	100	91	50	83	25	349	46.40
7. Rexona	125	114	100	91	50	480	63.82
8. Breeze	90	50	60	20	16	236	31.38
9. Dove	15	2	10	19	15	61	8.11
10. Palmolive	19	20	15	23	5	82	10.9
11. Pears	50	40	17	51	19	177	23.53
12. Paris	15	10		10	13	48	6.38
13. No. 1	25	10	4	3	15	57	7.57
14. Margo	15	11	5	15		46	6.11
15. GIV	12	3	4	7	10	36	4.78
16. Savlon	10	5	3	6		24	3.19
17. Dettol	52	20	40	35	13	160	21.27
18. Camay	5	4	10	16	2	37	4.92
19. Rose	4	3	2		5	14	1.86
20. Amway	4	10	2			16	2.12
21. Hamam	15	30	35	40	7	127	16.88
22. Fa		5	2	12	2	21	2.79
23. MediMix	3			10		13	1.72
24. Neem	2	2	1	7		12	1.59
25. Jay	1	4	1	2		8	1.06
26. Others	8			2	2	12	1.59

Note: Others constitute 9 less known brands i.e. Ayush, Marvel, Nikhar, Denim, Climix, Imperial Leather, Natural Sanifresh, and Fairlovely.

It is clear from the above table that Lux brand of toilet soap has the highest awareness level as it is indicated by 752 respondents out of 752 respondents i.e., 100%. Lifebuoy, Cinthol, Liril and Beauty are in 2nd , 3rd, 4th and 5th position with 98%, 96.40%, 74.6% and 73.93% respectively.

2. ***Sources of Information***

Consumers come to know about the brand of toilet soap which they are using from various sources such as personal sources, commercial sources, public sources and experimental sources. Personal sources consist of family, friends, neighbours, acquaintances etc. Commercial sources include salesperson, dealers, packaging, displays, etc. Public sources constitute TV, radio, newspapers, magazines etc. and experimental sources include handling, examining, using the product, etc. Identification and evaluation of the relative importance of the various sources is very important to the marketers for preparing the effective communication for the target market. Information collected on this issue has been shown in Table 50.

Table 50
Sources of information in making purchase decision of toilet soap

	No. of Respondents						
Soures Category	*Bishnupur*	*Thoubal*	*Imphal East*	*Imphal West*	*Church-andpur*	*Total*	*Per-centage*
a. Family/ Friends/ Neighbour	25	41	83	37	31	217	28.85
b. Sales person/ Retailer/ Packaging! Signboards/ Posters	33	24	22	43	10	132	17.55
c. TV/Radio/ Newspaper/ Magazine	83	56	34	81	45	299	39.76
d. Handling/ Examining/ Using the product	32	30	12	18	12	104	13.82
Total	173	151	151	179	98	752	100

It is evident from the above table that the public sources are the main sources of consumers' information as they are indicated by 299 respondents out of 752. The personal sources of information are in the second place as they are indicated by 28.85% of the respondents. The third place is occupied by commercial sources with 17.55%. Experimental sources of information are in the 4th place with 13.82% of respondents indicating it as the sources of information from which they come to know about the brands of toilet soap. Public sources are the main sources of information in Bishnupur, Thoubal and Churchandpur districts whereas personal source are the main sources of information in Churchandpur district.

3. *Product Factors*

Consumers usually evaluate the brands available with the help of information as they try to find out which brand will satisfy their needs. Consumer sees each product as a bundle of attributes with varying capabilities of delivering the sought benefits. Consumers purchase that particular brand which delivers the benefits sought by them. The benefits sought by the consumers in a particular brand are being referred to as product factors for the purpose of the study.

An enquiry is made in this regard to find out three main benefits sought by consumers by putting a question to the respondents. The respondents are asked to tick three main benefits from among the given probable benefits related to toilet soap. The responses so collected are computed in the Table 51.

It is clear from the Table 51 that the three main benefits sought by the respondents are freshness / deodorant, health / germ protection and skin care which constitute 21.36%, 20.47% and 17.64% of responses respectively. Further, it is also revealed that the district-wise three main benefits sought by the respondents are as under.

Table 51
Product factors (benefits sought) in consumer's choice of toilet soap

Soures Category	*No. of Respondents*					*Total*	*Per-centage*
	Bishnupur	*Thoubal*	*Imphal East*	*Imphal West*	*Church-andpur*		
a. Health/germ protection	95	117	70	107	73	462	20.47
b. Beauty / Glamour	95	53	62	90	27	327	14.49
c. Freshness / Deodorant	83	104	110	106	79	482	21.36
d. Economy / Lowerprice	91	55	90	87	17	340	15.07
e. Skin care	85	100	50	92	71	398	17.64
f. Durability	70	24	71	55	27	247	10.94
Total	519	453	453	537	294	2256	100

Table 52
District wise three main benefits sought by the consumers of toilet soap

Districts	*3 main benefits sought*
Bishnupur	Health/germ protection, beauty/glamour and economy/lower price
Thoubal	Health/germ protection, freshness/deodorant and skin care
Imphal East	Freshness/deodorant, economy/lower price and durability
Imphal West	Health/germ protection, freshness/deodorant and skin care
Churchandpur	Freshness/deodorant, Health/germ protection and skincare

4. *Marketing factors*

Marketers, generally, use various means or strategies in their attempt to get positive response from the consumers to whom they are targeting. For the purpose of the present study, the strategies adopted by the marketers are being referred to as marketing factors. An attempt is made to determine three main factors to which consumers of toilet soap are likely to have positive response. Out of the 13 marketing factors considered for the study, respondents are asked to indicate three main important factors which influence them in the selection of the brand of toilet soap. The picture that emerges from the responses has been presented in the Table 53.

Table 53
Marketing factors in the consumer's choice of a particular brand of toilet soap

	No. of Respondents District-wise					
Marketing Factor	*Bishnupur*	*Thoubal*	*Imphal East*	*Imphal West*	*Church-andpur*	*Total*
a. Product benefits	106	90	70	126	20	412
b. Product variety	7	7	10	20	8	52
c. Durability	10	8	5	15	31	69
d. Free gift offer	40	80	40	50	33	243
e. Attractivepackaging	11	9	19	25	15	79
f. Size	10	8	5	15	6	44
g. Lower price/ economy	70	30	33	50	19	202
h. Discount	13	20	33	20	25	111
i. Advertizing	92	83	70	65	47	357
j. Popularity of brand	65	50	55	33	31	234
K. Extensive availability	6	10	15	18	17	66
l. Availability at exclusive outlet (Such as cosmetic store)	4	3	18	5	2	32
m. Recommendation of retailer	85	55	80	95	40	355
Total	519	453	453	537	294	2256

Note: Product benefits include germ protection, beauty, freshness and skin care.

It is evident from the above table that the three main marketing factors which influence the consumers in their buying decision are product benefits, advertising and recommendation of retailers as the total responses of each of these factors are higher than that of other factors. Total responses of each of the main factors mentioned above are 412, 357 and 355 respectively out of the total responses of 2256. The district-wise three main factors influencing consumers' decisions are given as below.

Table 54
District-wise three main marketing factors

Districts	*3 main marketing factors*
Bishnupur	Product benefit, advertising and recommendation of retailers.
Thoubal	Product benefit, advertising and free gift offer
Imphal East	Recommendation of retailer, product benefit and advertising
Imphal West	Product benefit, recommendation of retailer and Advertising
Churchandpur	Advertising, recommendation of retailer and free gift offer

5. *Buying Roles*

People play different roles in buying decisions. They may be initiators, influencers, deciders, buyers and users. In order to ascertain the roles played by respondents in their buying decisions of toilet soap, questions are served to them. Responses received from them are presented in the tables numbering 55, 56, 57, 58 and 59.

Initiator

It is evident from the following Table 55 that youngsters (37.23%) are the main initiators in the purchase of a particular brand of toilet soap. Mother (30.58%), as the initiator, is placed in the second position. Adults with 13.29% of the total respondents occupy the third position. In all the districts, the main initiators are also youngsters in the family.

Table 55
Initiators in the purchase of a particular brand of toilet soap district-wise

	No. of Respondents District-wise						
Initiator Category	*Bishnupur*	*Thoubal*	*Imphal East*	*Imphal West*	*Churchandpur*	*Total*	*Percentage*
a. Children (below 15 years of age)	14	3	3	6	3	29	3.85
b. Youngsters (age between 15 and 25 yrs)	57	60	60	80	23	280	37.23
c. Adults (unmarried and newly married persons)	30	27	22	11	10	100	13.29
d. Parents (persons having dependent children) F	11	14	5	9	3	42	5.98
M	41	47	45	49	48	230	30.58
e. Elders (persons having grand children)	15		13	17	8	53	7.04
f. Any member of the family	5		3	7	3	18	2.39
g. Total	173	151	151	179	98	752	100

Note: F stands for father and M stands for mother.

Influencer

Neighbours, relatives and friends are the main influencers in the choice of a particular brand of toilet soap. This is indicated by 411 respondents out of the total of 752 respondents i.e. 54.65%. Co-workers and colleagues (17.42%) are placed in the second place as influencers which is followed by retailers with 9.97%. In all the districts, the main influencers are also the neighbours, relatives and friends. The above description has been presented in Table 56.

Table 56
Influencers in the purchase of a particular brand of toilet soap

	No. of Respondents District-wise						
Initiator Category	*Bishnupur*	*Thoubal*	*Imphal East*	*Imphal West*	*Church-andpur*	*Total*	*Per-centage*
a. Coworkers/ colleagues	20	44	20	57	23	164	21.8
b. Neighbours/ relatives/ friends	99	73	107	82	50	411	54.65
c. Retailers	23	4	14	17	17	75	9.97
d. Members of clubs/ associations where respondents belongs to	8	6	2	10	3	29	3.85
e. Any other	23	24	8	13	5	73	9.7
Total	173	151	151	179	98	752	100

Note: Advertisement through TV, Radio, Newspaper, magazines and billboards are included in any other category.

Decider

The information collected from respondents as depicted in Table 57 speaks clearly that mother is the main decider in the selection of a particular brand of toilet soap. The second place is occupied by the youngsters (28.05%). The decider category "any members of the family" with 17.20% is placed in the third position as decider. In addition, mother is also the main decider in all the districts.

Table 57
Final decider in the selection of a particular brand of toilet soap

	No. of Respondents District-wise						
Decider Category	*Bishnupur*	*Thoubal*	*Imphal East*	*Imphal West*	*Church-andpur*	*Total*	*Per-centage*
a. Children (below 15 years of age)		2		2	3	7	0.93
b. Youngsters (age between 15 and 25 yrs)	43	42	45	49	32	211	28.05
c. Adults (unmarried and newly married persons)	25	26	19	10	10	90	11.96
d. Parents (Persons having dependent children) F		7	6	7	3	23	3.05
M	48	53	45	65	39	250	33.24
e. Elders (Persons having grand children)	16		3	15	7	41	5.54
f. Any member of the family	41	21	33	31	4	130	17.28
g. Total	173	151	151	179	98	752	100

Note: F stands for father and M stands for mother

Buyer

Buyers are the people who make the actual purchase. It is indicated from the Table 58 that the buyer category "Any member of the family" which constitute 36.96% share of the buyers is the main buyer of the toilet soap. This is followed by mother with 28.05% and children with 9.84%.

Table 58
Buyers of the toilet soap

		No. of Respondents District-wise						
Buyers Category		*Bishnupur*	*Thoubal*	*Imphal East*	*Imphal West*	*Church-andpur*	*Total*	*Per-centage*
a. Children (below 15 years)		17	20	14	19	4	74	9.84
b. Youngsters (age between 15 and 25 yrs)		14	9	16	15	9	63	8.37
c. Adults (unmarried and newly married persons)		21	15	13	8	9	66	8.77
d. Parents (person shaving dependent children)	F		8		10	3	21	2.79
	M	33	45	43	52	38	211	28.05
e. Elders (persons having grand children)		14		10	5	4	33	4.38
f. Any member of the family		74	54	55	64	31	278	36.96
g. Total		173	151	151	179	98	752	100

Note: F stands for father and M stands for mother.

User

As far as the other users in the family of the same brand as that of the respondents are concerned, the category of "all the members of the family" is placed in the first position with 75.93%. This is followed by parents and brothers with 6.91 % and 4.52% respectively. The above description has been presented in the Table 59.

Table 59
Other members of the family who use the same brand of toilet soap as that of the respondents.

	No. of Respondents District-wise						
Users Category	*Bishnupur*	*Thoubal*	*Imphal East*	*Imphal West*	*Church-andpur*	*Total*	*Per-centage*
a. Parents	11	8	11	5	17	52	6.91
b. Elders	2	2	3	2	6	15	1.99
c. Brothers	7	2	8	6	11	34	4.52
d. Sisters	4	2	8	5	9	28	3.72
e. Husband	5	1	—	7	3	16	2.12
f. Wife	6	11	8	11	—	36	4.78
g. Any members of the family	138	125	113	143	52	571	75.93
Total	173	151	151	179	98	752	100

6. *Consumer's preferable (use) brand of toilet soap*

In all, there are thirty-eight brands of toilet soaps which are available in Manipur. But it is only 33 brands (excluding Amway products) of toilet soap which are found to be used by the respondents. Among these brands, Cinthol is the brand, which has maximum number of respondents purchasing it and using it. Cinthol occupies first place as it is used by 114 respondents out of 572 i.e.15.15%. Lux, Beauty, Lifebuoy brands are in second, third and fourth place with 13.03%, 12.36% and 9.57% share respectively.

Other brands of toilet soap are not so much significantly used by the respondents. Further, Beauty brand is the brand of toilet soap which has the highest use in Bishnupur, Imphal East and Churchandpur district whereas Lux has the highest use in Thoubal. And Cinthol has the highest use in Imphal West district. The whole information mentioned above is presented in the following Table 60.

Table 60

Consumer's preferable (use) brand of toilet soap

	No. of Respondents District-wise						
Name of the Brands	*Bishnupur*	*Thoubal*	*Imphal East*	*Imphal West*	*Church-andpur*	*Total*	*Per-centage*
1. Cinthol	21	26	20	36	11	114	15.15
2. Lux	13	30	23	22	10	98	13.03
3. Beauty	31	11	30	8	13	93	12.36
4. Lifebouy	16	13	19	15	9	72	9.57
5. Liril	7	13	17	8	9	54	7.18
6. Nirma	14	19	3	8	5	49	6.51
7. Rexona	8	3	9	9	8	37	4.92
8. Breeze	12	5	7	6	3	33	4.38
9. Dove	5		6	15	6	32	4.25
10. Palmolive	3	8	4	14	2	31	4.12
11. Pears	2	2	7	6	4	21	2.79
12. Paris	11	6		2	2	21	2.79
13. No. 1	9	1			4	14	1.86
14. Margo	4	2	1	7		14	1.86
15. GIV	2			1	5	8	1.06
16. Savlon	5	1		2		8	1.06
17. Dettol	1		2	5		8	1.06
18. Camay	1	1	1	4		7	0.93
19. Rose	1	1			3	5	0.66
20. Amway	1	4				5	0.66
21. Hamam		2	1	2		5	0.66
22. Fa		1		2	2	5	0.66
23. Medimix	1			3		4	0.53
24. Neem			1	2		3	0.39
25. Jay		2				2	0.26
26. Others	5			2	2	9	1.19
Total	173	151	151	179	98	752	100

Note: Other brands consist of 9 brands of toilet soap. They are Ayush, Marvel, Nikhar, Denim, Clinics, Imperal Leather, Natural, Sanifresh and Fairlovely.

Majority of the consumers frequently buy their toilet soap from nearby general stores. It is clear from the Table 61 given below that 358 out of 752 respondents i.e. 47.60% buy toilet soap from the nearby general stores. And 24.10%, 13.56% and 11.17% of respondents purchase their toilet soap frequently from main market general stores, main market cosmetic stores and nearby pan dukan respectively.

Any other outlet constitutes a small 3.59% of respondents and they purchase their toilet soap from where so ever it is available. They do not stick to any particular type of outlet. In addition, in all the districts majority of the respondents purchase their toilet soap from nearby general store.

Table 61
Consumer's choice of outlets (toilet soap)

	No. of Respondents District-wise						
Outlet Category	*Bishnupur*	*Thoubal*	*Imphal East*	*Imphal West*	*Church-andpur*	*Total*	*Per-centage*
a. Nearby General Store	58	77	83	100	40	358	47.60
b. Main market General store	55	27	31	37	31	181	24.06
c. Nearby Pan Dukan	28	24	15	8	9	84	11.17
d. Main Market Cosmetic store	16	16	22	32	16	102	13.56
e. Any Other	16	7		2	2	27	3.59
Total	173	151	151	179	98	752	100

8. ***Purchase Amount***

Majority of the consumers i.e., 239 respondents out of 752 respondents purchase a piece of toilet soap at a time. This constitutes 31.78% of the respondents. Three pieces, two pieces, a dozen, six pieces, and four pieces respectively are purchased by 17.42%, 17.28%, 15.02%, 9.44% and 9.04% of respondents. Moreover, consumers mainly purchase 3 pieces and 4 pieces of toilet soap at a time when the companies offer 2+ 1 and 3+ 1 schemes respectively. In all the districts, majority of the respondents purchase one piece of toilet soap at a time. The above information is depicted in the following Table 62.

Table 62
Consumer's purchase amount (toilet soap)

Purchase amount Category	*No. of Respondents District-wise*					*Total*	*Per-centage*
	Bishnupur	*Thoubal*	*Imphal East*	*Imphal West*	*Church-andpur*		
a. One	44	60	69	38	28	239	31.78
b. Two	14	37	30	29	20	130	17.28
c. Three	40	26	16	28	21	131	17.42
d. Four	22	9	12	20	5	68	9.04
e. Six	15	10	7	33	6	71	9.44
f. Dozen	38	9	17	31	18	113	15.02
Total	173	151	151	179	98	752	100

9. ***Consumer's satisfaction with the brand presently in use***

Consumer's satisfaction in the brand which he is using is very important. As a matter of fact a consumer is satisfied only when his expectations are delivered by the product / brand. A consumer who is dissatisfied, usually, shifts to the other brands. An attempt is made to have an idea whether the consumers are satisfied or dissatisfied with the brand of toilet soap, which they are presently using. The picture that emerges from the responses has been presented in the Table 63.

Table 63
Consumer's satisfaction / dissatisfaction with the brand of toilet soap presently in use

Response Category	*No. of Respondents District-wise*					*Total*	*Per-centage*
	Bishnupur	*Thoubal*	*Imphal East*	*Imphal West*	*Church-andpur*		
a. Satisfied	166	149	148	164	91	718	95.4
b. Dissatisfied	7	2	3	15	7	34	4.52
Total	173	151	151	179	98	752	100

The above table clearly shows that 718 respondents out of 752 respondents i.e. 95.4% are satisfied with the brand they are presently using whereas 4.52% of the respondents are dissatisfied. The reasons for dissatisfaction include high price, non-durability of the soap, and frequent non-availability of a particular brand of choice.

10. ***Brand Loyalty***

Some consumers are loyal to the brand of product, which they are using and some are not. But the buyers who are brand loyal tend not to change their buying pattern as a result of competitive promotion. Moreover, a brand loyal buyer when he does not get the brand of his choice in a particular shop he goes to the other shop in search of the brand of his choice.

In this regard, a question was put to the respondents. The responses collected are given in the following Table 64.

Table 64
Step taken by the respondents when the brand of toilet soap of their choice is not available in a particular shop

	No. of Respondents District-wise						
Response Category	*Bishnupur*	*Thoubal*	*Imphal East*	*Imphal West*	*Church-andpur*	*Total*	*Per-centage*
a. Ask for anotherbrand of soap	26	32	106	140	37	341	45.34
b. Go to another shop to purchase the brand of hischoice	147	119	45	39	61	411	54.64
Total	173	151	151	179	98	752	100

It is evident from the Table 64 that 411 respondents out of 752 i.e. 54.64% go to another shop searching for the same brand of toilet soap of their choice whereas 341 respondents out of 752 i.e. 45.3% ask for another brand of toilet from the same shop when the brand of their choice is not available. This indicates that 54.64% of the buyers are brand loyal.

Moreover, out of the 5 districts of Manipur covered in the study, in three districts namely, Bishnupur, Thoubal and Churchandpur the number of buyers who are brand loyal is more than that of those who are not brand loyal. But in two districts, namely Imphal East and Imphal West the number of buyers who are not brand loyal is more than that of those who are brand loyal.

11. ***Types of buying behaviour***

Consumers exhibit different patterns of buying behaviour depending upon the degree of consumer involvement and the degree of difference among the brands. With a view to have a peep into the types of buying behaviour that are associated with the purchase of toilet soap, questions are put to the respondents in respect of the involvement of other members of the family and respondent's perceived difference in the quality among the brands of toilet soap available in the market. Responses so collected are tabulated in the following tables numbering 65 and 66.

Involvement of other members of the family

Table 65
Involvement of other members of the family in the purchase of a particular brand of toilet soap

	No. of Respondents District-wise						
Response Category	*Bishnupur*	*Thoubal*	*Imphal East*	*Imphal West*	*Church-andpur*	*Total*	*Per-centage*
a. Involvement	153	131	107	141	35	567	75.39
b. No involvement	20	20	44	38	63	185	24.6
Total	173	151	151	179	98	752	100

The Table 65 depicts that 567 respondents out of 752 i.e. 75.39% involve other members of the family in the purchase of a particular brand of toilet soap whereas 24.60% of respondents feel that there is no involvement of the other members of the family. It is also seen from the above table that Churchandpur district is the only district in which the number of the respondents indicating involvement of other members of the family in the choice of toilet soap is less than that of no involvement.

Buyer's perception of brand difference

Out of 752 respondents, 713 i.e. 94.89% feel that there is significant difference among the available brands of toilet soap. And 5.18% of the respondents feel that there is no significant difference among the available brands. The information mentioned above is presented in the following Table 66.

Table 66
Buyer's perception of significant difference among the available brands of toilet soap

	No. of Respondents District-wise						
Response Category	*Bishnupur*	*Thoubal*	*Imphal East*	*Imphal West*	*Church-andpur*	*Total*	*Per-centage*
a. Significant difference	170	147	143	176	77	713	94.81
b. No significant difference	3	4	8	3	21	39	5.18
Total	173	151	151	179	98	752	100

Types of buying behaviour

A further deep look into the responses reveals that the number of respondents who indicate involvement and significant difference among the brand is 549. The number of respondents who indicate no involvement and significant difference among the brand is 164. Involvement and no significant difference among the brand is indicated by 18 respondents. And the number of respondents who indicate no involvement and no significant difference is 21. The above description is presented in the following Table 67.

Table 67
Involvement vis-à-vis brand difference

Degree of perceived Brand difference	*No. of respondents Degree of involvement*		*Total*
	Involvement	*No Involvement*	
Significant Brand difference	549	164	713
No Significant Brand difference	18	21	39
Total	567	185	752

It may be seen from the table that 549 respondents out of 752 i.e. 73% exhibit complex buying behaviour. 18 respondents out of 752 i.e. 2.39% exhibit dissonance reducing buying behaviour. Variety seeking buying behaviour is associated with 164 out of 752 respondents i.e., 21.80%. And habitual buying behaviour is manifested by 21 respondents out of 752 i.e.2.79%.

Consumer Buying Behaviour of Durable Goods (TV)

Durable goods are the tangible goods that normally survive many uses. TV receiver or TV set belongs to the durable goods category. TV has become an essential household item for watching entertainment programmes, educational programmes, news, etc. Purchase of TV is a high involvement decision. Since a TV set is bought very infrequently and typically once or twice in one's life time, consumers think a lot before making purchase decision. Consumer buying behaviour of TV is being discussed in this part of the chapter.

This portion covers the following aspects:

i) Consumer's awareness level of different brands
ii) Consumer's sources of information
iii) Product factors and marketing factors involved in the choice of a particular brand
iv) Buying roles.
v) Preferable (use) brands of TV, outlets of purchase, modes of purchase and purchase occasions.
vi) Consumer's satisfaction with the brands of TV presently in use.
vii) Brand loyalty
viii) Types of buying behaviour.

1. ***Consumer's awareness level of different brands of TV***

All the marketers try to create awareness of their products in the minds of the consumers. For achieving this purpose, lakhs of rupees were spent by the companies in advertising and sales promotional activities. As a matter of fact, product trial rate is related with awareness level. Moreover, awareness is the first step in the adoption process i.e. awareness, interest, evaluation, trial and adoption. In order to determine the awareness level of TV, information was collected in this aspect and presented in the following Table 6.

Table 68
Consumer's awareness level of different brands of TV

	No. of Respondents District-wise						
Name of the Brands	*Bishnupur*	*Thoubal*	*Imphal East*	*Imphal West*	*Church-andpur*	*Total*	*Per-centage*
1	*2*	*3*	*4*	*5*	*6*	*7*	*8*
1. Onida	173	151	151	179	98	752	100
2. Sony	161	123	151	179	91	705	93.75
3. Philips	173	151	151	179	98	752	100

(Contd....)

1	*2*	*3*	*4*	*5*	*6*	*7*	*8*
4. Videocon	157	142	145	169	79	692	92.05
5. Manitron	173	151	151	179	98	752	100
6. L.G	122	131	138	153	69	613	81.51
7. AIWA	125	134	143	161	53	616	91.91
8. BPL	129	137	151	163	59	639	84.97
9. Akai	117	122	139	149	47	574	76.32
10. Thomson	100	97	89	121	38	445	59.17
11. Sansui	76	55	78	95	27	331	44.01
12. Beltex	81	61	71	67	23	303	40.29
13. Weston	33	24	56	48	12	173	23
14. Sangai	56	33	52	59	23	223	29.65
15. T-Series	35	45	51	53	18	202	26.86
16. Oscar	15	31	13	15	17	91	12.10
17. Samsung	15	17	18	17	12	79	10.50
18. Nelco	9	5	3	10	12	39	5.18
19. Salora	9	15	13	12	11	60	7.97
20. Konka	5	8	3	7	2	25	3.32
21. Telerama	5	7	4	3	2	21	2.79
22. Bush	10	8	5	4	2	29	3.85
23. Televesta	6	5	3	5	3	22	2.92
24. Texla	5	2	3	4	2	16	2.12
25. Dynora	2	3	5	7	8	25	3.32
26. DTV	5	2	2	2	2	13	1.72
Others	5	8		9		22	2.92

Note: 1 Others include 12 less known brands. They are Binaton, Panasonic, Vista vision, Orson, Keltron, Kono, Tulsi, Hitachi, Haggaline, Etxt, Uptron and Supertron.

2 For measuring the awareness level of different brands of TV, information from the total responses of 752 was taken. But, for analysing the other aspects of consumer buying behaviour of TV, information from 603 respondents (TV owners only) was taken.

It is seen from the above table that Onida, Philips and Manitron brands of TV have cent percent awareness. This is followed by Sony brand and Videocon brand with 93.75% and 92.05% of respondents respectively. Further, it is observed that Sony brand has cent percent awareness in Imphal East and Imphal West districts and BPL has cent percent awareness in Imphal East district.

2. *Sources of Information*

For preparing an effective communication for the target market, identification and evaluation of the relative importance of the various sources of information is very important to the marketers.

Various sources from which consumers come to know about the brand of TV which they own are personal sources, commercial sources, public sources and experimental sources. Personal sources constitute family, friends, neighbours, acquaintances etc. Commercial sources include salesperson, dealers, packaging, displays, etc. Public sources comprise TV, radio, newspapers, magazines etc. and Experimental sources include handling, examining, using the product, etc. Information gathered in this aspect has been tabulated in the Table 69.

Table 69
Sources of information in making purchase decision of TV

	No. of Respondents District-wise						
Respondent's Category	*Bishnupur*	*Thoubal*	*Imphal East*	*Imphal West*	*Churchandpur*	*Total*	*Percentage*
a. Family/ Friends/ Neighbour	47	38	42	38	16	181	30.01
b. Sales person/ Retailer/ Packaging/ Signboards/ Posters	28	6	6	27	6	73	12.10
c. TV/Radio/ Magazine	83	60	68	77	26	314	52.07
d. Handling/ Examining/ Using the product	4	15	5	6	5	35	5.80
Total	162	119	121	148	53	603	100

The above table depicts that the public sources of information occupy the highest share of information from which TV owners come to know the brand of TV which they are using.

Public sources constitute 52.07% of the respondents (TV owners). This is followed by Personal sources with 30.01 % of the respondents. The third place is occupied by Commercial sources with 12.10%. Further, public sources of information are also the main consumer's sources of information in all the districts.

3. *Product Factors*

With the help of information from various sources, consumers evaluate the brands available as they try to find out the brand that will satisfy their needs. The benefits sought by the consumers in a particular brand are being referred to as product factors for the purpose of the study. Consumers usually purchase that particular brand which delivers the benefits sought by them. An investigation is carried out in this regard to find out three main benefits sought by the consumers by putting a question to respondents. Respondents are asked to tick three main benefits from among the given probable benefits related to TV. The responses so collected are computed in Table 70.

Table 70
Product factors (benefits sought) in consumer's choice of a TV brand

	No. of Respondents District-wise						
Respondent's Category	*Bishnupur*	*Thoubal*	*Imphal East*	*Imphal West*	*Churchandpur*	*Total*	*Percentage*
1	*2*	*3*	*4*	*5*	*6*	*7*	*8*
a. Picture quality	108	77	70	105	45	405	22.38
b. Sound quality	87	40	50	75	43	295	16.30

(Contd....)

1	*2*	*3*	*4*	*5*	*6*	*7*	*8*
c. Remote control	28	16	25	25	10	104	5.74
d. Picture in pictures	3	11	16	3	3	36	1.99
e. Durability	52	45	54	72	17	240	13.26
f. Brand image		2	3	2	8	15	0.82
g. Less (economic) price	43	34	30	40	5	152	8.40
h. External features (looks)	5		1	2	4	12	0.66
1. Programming of channel	26	15	20	20	5	86	4.75
J. Auto channel	31	14	18	25	4	92	5.08
k. Child lock					5	5	0.27
1. Warranty	61	52	51	40	7	211	11.66
m. Easy installment scheme	42	51	25	35	3	156	8.62
Total	486	357	363	444	159	1809	100

It is evident from the above table that the three main benefits sought by the consumers in the choice of a particular TV are picture quality, sound quality, and durability which constitute 22.38%, 16.30%, and 13.26% of the total responses respectively. Further, it is also seen that the district-wise three main benefits sought by the respondents are as under.

Table 71

District-wise three main benefits sought by the consumers of TV

Districts	*3 main benefits sought*
Bishnupur	Picture quality, sound quality, and warranty
Thoubal	Picture quality, warranty and easy instalments scheme
Imphal East	Picture quality, durability and warranty
Imphal West	Picture quality, sound quality, and durability
Churchandpur	Picture quality, sound quality, and durability

4. *Marketing factors*

Consumers respond differently to the marketing

strategies adopted by the marketers. It is, therefore, imperative for the marketers to identify the means or the strategies to which the consumers are responding positively. For the purpose of the present study, the strategies or the means adopted by the marketers in order to get positive response from the consumers are being referred to as marketing factors. An attempt is made to determine three main factors to which consumers of TV are likely to have positive response. Of the 14 marketing factors considered for the study, respondents are asked to indicate three main important factors, which influence them in the selection of the brand of TV. The responses so collected are computed in the Table 72.

Table 72
Marketing factors in the consumer's choice of a particular brand of TV

Marketing Factor	*No of Respondents – District-wise*					Per-centage
	Bishnupur	*Thoubal*	*Imphal East*	*Imphal West*	*Churchand-pur*	
a. Product benefits	84	76	75	98	40	373
b. Durability	43	30	42	12	20	147
C. Free gift offer	19	7	5	8	6	45
d. External features	20	7	5	13	4	49
e. Size	33	4	7	10	1	55
f. Lower (economic) price	56	29	31	50	3	169
g. Discount	4	7	4	3	4	22
h. Advertising	70	51	71	49	34	275
i. Popularity of band	29	3	6	13	6	57
j. Extensive availability	3	5	2	25	6	41
k. Recommendation of dealers	29	20	30	33	23	135
l. Warranty	46	68	50	75	10	249
m. After sales service	7					7
n. Easy installment scheme	50	43	35	55	2	185
Others	486	357	363	444	159	1809

Note: Product benefits include picture quality, sound quality, picture in picture, auto channel selection, remote control, programming of channels, etc.

It is observed from the above table that the three main marketing factors which influence the consumers in their buying decision are product benefits, advertising and warranty. The total responses of each of these factors are higher than that of other factors.

The product benefit, advertising and warranty factors have the total responses of 373, 275 and 249 respectively out of the total of 1809. The district-wise three main factors influencing the consumer's decisions are given as below.

Table 73
District-wise three main marketing factors

Districts	*3 main marketing factors*
Bishnupur	Product benefits, advertising and lower (economic) price.
Thoubal	Product benefits, warranty and advertising
Imphal East	Product benefits, advertising and easy instalments scheme
Imphal West	Product benefits, warranty and easy instalments scheme
Churchandpur	Product benefits, advertising, recommendation of dealers

5. ***Buying Roles***

People play different roles such as initiators, influencers, deciders, buyers and users in buying decision.

In order to determine the roles played by respondents in their buying decision of TV, questions are put to respondents in the questionnaire. Responses collected from them are computed in the tables numbering 74, 75, 76 and 77.

Initiator

It is clear from Table 74 that mother who constitutes 33.33% is the main initiator in the purchase of a particular brand of TV. Youngster (26.53%) as initiator is placed in the second position. Father with 23.38% is placed in the third position. Further, mother is the main initiator in the districts of Bishnupur and Thoubal whereas father is the main initiator in the districts of Imphal East, Imphal West and Churchandpur district.

Table 74

Initiators in the purchase of a particular brand of TV

Initiator Category	*No. of Respondents District-Wise*						
	Bishnupur	*Thoubal*	*Imphal East*	*Imphal West*	*Church-andpur*	*Total*	*Per-centage*
a. Children (below 15 years of age)	4	6		2	9	21	3.48
b. Youngsters (age between 15 and 25 yrs)	47	27	34	41	11	160	26.53
c. Adults (unmarried and newly married persons)	14	11	15	16	4	60	9.95
d. Parents (persons having dependent children) F	23	16	36	50	16	141	23.38
M	70	59	30	31	11	201	33.33
e. Elders (persons having grand children)	4		6	8	2	20	3.31
f. Total	162	119	121	148	53	603	100

Note: F stands for father and M stands for mother.

Influencer

The main influencers in the choice of a particular brand of TV are neighbours, relatives and friends. This constitutes

44.11 % of the respondents. Co- workers and colleagues with 34.66% of the respondents are placed in the second position. Dealers with 15.92% of respondents are placed in third position. The main influencers in all the districts except Bishnupur district are neighbours, relatives and friends. In Bishnupur district main influencers are co-workers and colleagues. The above description is based on the information presented in Table 75.

Table 75
Influencers in the purchase of a particular brand of TV

	No. of Respondents District-wise						
Initiator Category	*Bishnupur*	*Thoubal*	*Imphal East*	*Imphal West*	*Church-andpur*	*Total*	*Per-centage*
a. Coworkers/ colleagues	84	35	42	45	3	209	34.66
b. Neighbours/ relatives	56	49	52	80	29	266	44.11
c. Dealers	16	30	21	13	16	96	15.92
d. Any other	6	5	6	10	5	32	5.30
Total	162	119	121	148	53	603	100

Note: Advertisement through TV, Radio, Newspapers, magazines and billboards are included in any other category.

Decider

Father as final decider in the choice of a particular brand of TV is placed in the first position as it is indicated by 40.29% of the respondents. This is followed by mother with 27.52%. Youngsters with 13.26% are placed in the third position. Further, in all the districts, father is also the main decider in the choice of a particular brand of TV. The above description is indicted from the information presented in Table 76.

Table 76
Final decider in the selection of a particular brand of TV

Decider Category	*No. of Respondents District-wise* Bishnupur	Thoubal	Imphal East	Imphal West	Church-andpur	*Total*	*Per-centage*
a. Youngsters (age between 15 and 25 years)	18	16	17	25	4	80	13.26
b. Adults (unmarried and newly married persons)	13	13	12	21	3	62	10.28
c. Parents (persons having dependent children) F	72	52	39	49	31	243	40.29
M	46	35	38	39	8	166	27.52
d. Elders (persons having grand children)	5		7	8		20	3.31
e. All the members of the family	8	3	8	6	7	32	5.30
f. Total	162	119	121	148	53	603	100

Note: F stands for father and M stands for mother.

Buyers

Father as buyer of TV occupies the highest share of buyers who makes the actual purchase. Father as buyer constitutes 59.36%. This is followed by youngsters with 15.09%. Third place is occupied by adult with 13.10%. Further, father is also the main buyer in all the districts. The above description is presented in Table 77.

Table 77
Buyers of TV

Buyer Category		*No. of Respondents District-wise*						
		Bishnupur	*Thoubal*	*Imphal East*	*Imphal West*	*Church-andpur*	*Total*	*Per-centage*
a. Youngsters (Age between 15 and 25 yrs)		27	15	19	26	4	91	15.09
b. Adults (Unmarried and newly married persons)		20	16	19	21	3	79	13.10
c. Parents (Persons having dependent children)	F	101	82	57	74	44	358	59.36
	M	9	6	19	19		53	8.78
d. Elders (Persons having grand children)		5		7	8	2	22	3.64
e. Total		162	119	121	148	53	603	100

Note: F stands for father and M stands for mother,

6. *Consumer's preferable (use) brand of TV*

This aspect of consumer behaviour covers the brands of TV which are owned and used by the respondents. Other brands, if any, used by the other members of the family are covered in the Chapter 3. It is evident from the Table 78 that there are 38 brands of TV owned by the respondents in the five districts of Manipur covered for the study. Among these brands, Onida is the brand which has maximum number of respondents who have owned the brand. Onida brand occupies the first place in ownership as it is owned by 96 respondents out of 603 respondents (TV owners) i.e., 15.92%

Sony occupies the second place with 12.93% of the respondents owning it. Philips and Videocon with 12.10% each occupy the third place. The fourth place is occupied by the local made brand "Manitron" with 9.78% ownership.

Table 78
Consumer's preferable (use) brands of TV

	No. of Respondents District-wise						
Name of the Brand	*Bishnupur*	*Thoubal*	*Imphal East*	*Imphal West*	*Church-andpur*	*Total*	*Per-centage*
1. Onida	23	24	17	21	11	96	15.92
2. Sony	22	14	7	20	15	78	12.93
3. Philips	21	17	6	23	6	73	12.10
4. Videpcon	20	20	18	13	2	73	12.10
5. Manitron	25	3	14	12	5	59	9.78
6. L.G.	5	1	16	10	5	37	6.13
7. AIWA	11	7	9	5	2	34	5.63
8. BPL	6	4	9	7	1	27	4.47
9. Akai	3	1	7	13		24	3.98
10. Thomson		2	8	2	2	14	2.32
11. Sansui	3	5	1	2		11	1.82
12. Beltex	3	2	3	2		10	1.65
13. Weston	1	8				9	1.49
14. Sangai	2		5			7	1.16
15. T-Series	2	4				6	0.99
16. Oscar	1	1	1	2		5	0.82
17. Samsung	1			2	2	5	0.82
18. Nelco	1			2		3	0.49
19. Salora	2				2	3	0.49
20. Konka		1		2		3	0.49
21. Telerama	2			1		3	0.49
22. Bush	1	2				3	0.49
23. Telvista				2		2	0.33
24. Texla	2					2	0.33
25. Dynora				1	1	2	0.33
26. DTV	2					2	0.33
27. Others	3	3		6		12	1.99
Others	162	119	121	148	53	603	100

Note: Others include 12 less popular brands. They are Binaton, Panasonic, Vistavision, Orson, Keltron, Kono, Tulsi, Hitachi, Haqqaline, Etxt, Uptron, and Supertron.

7. ***Outlets of purchase***

Table 79
Outlets of purchase of TV

Buyer Category	No. of Respondents District-wise Bishnupur	Thoubal	Imphal East	Imphal West	Church-andpur	Total	Per-centage
a. Local dealer/agency	53	42	11	20	19	145	24.04
b. State capital	100	74	100	115	31	420	69.65
c. Outside state	9	3	10	13	3	38	6.30
Total	162	119	121	148	53	603	100

It is seen from the above table that majority of the consumers purchased their TV from the state capital Imphal as it is indicated by 69.65% of the respondents. This is followed by local dealer/agency with 24.04%.

8. ***Modes of purchase***

Table 80
Modes of purchase of TV

Mode of Purchase Category	No. of Respondents District-wise Bishnupur	Thoubal	Imphal East	Imphal West	Church-andpur	Total	Per-centage
1	*2*	*3*	*4*	*5*	*6*	*7*	*8*
a. Cash	96	52	76	69	35	328	54.39
b. Easy installment scheme	32	35	28	26	10	131	21.72

(Contd....)

1	*2*	*3*	*4*	*5*	*6*	*7*	*8*
c. Loan (borrowing money from others)	17	17	7	21	2	64	10.61
d. Through Marup (local scheme)	17	15	10	25	5	72	11.94
e. Through exchange scheme offer by thecompanies				7	1	8	1.32
Total	162	119	121	148	53	603	100

Note: Marup (Local Scheme) is a form of lottery in which every member of the Marup contributes a fixed amount of money every month and draws a lot. Total amount of money goes to the member who wins for the month. The same process follows in the next month but the name of the member who has already won will not be included for drawing a lot in the following months. This process continues till the lot covers all the members. The general rule is that in the time of giving the monthly contribution, members who have already won have to contribute their usual fixed contribution amount plus some interest fixed by the members of the marup. Thus, the one who receives at the end gets more money than those who received earlier.

It is evident from the above table that purchase of TV by cash constitutes the highest share of the mode of purchase with 54.39% of the respondents. This is followed by purchase mode "on easy instalments scheme given by dealers" with 21.72%. The third place is occupied by purchase mode through Marup (local scheme) with 11.94%.

9. *Purchase Occasions*

Buyers of TV can be distinguished according to occasions when they purchase a product. On the basis of this information marketer can develop appropriate marketing strategies to suit the occasions when consumers are most likely to purchase the product. Information regarding the occasions on which consumers of Manipur purchased their TV is given below.

Table 81
Purchase occasions of TV

	No. of Respondents District-wise						
Occasion Category	*Bishnupur*	*Thoubal*	*Imphal East*	*Imphal West*	*Church-andpur*	*Total*	*Per-centage*
a. During major international/ national sporting events	30	25	31	30	38	154	25.53
b. Diwali	6				2	8	1.32
c. Marriage Gift	30	36	21	45	9	141	23.38
d. Ningol Chakhouba gift	2	2		3		7	1.16
e. Any other occasions	94	56	69	53	4	293	48.59
Total	162	119	121	148	53	603	100

Note: Majority of the respondents who indicated the option "any other occasions" did not specify the occasion on which they purchased their TV sets.

It is observed from the above table that majority of the respondents indicated the option "Any other occasions". Any other occasions include when it is financially sound, New Year, birthday, any family occasions, when the family felt the necessity for having a TV set etc. Any other occasions is placed in the first place with 48.59% of the respondents indicating this option. Major international and National sporting events are placed in second place with 25.53%. Marriage gift option is placed in third placed with 23.38%.

10. *Consumer's satisfaction with the brand of TV presently in use*

A consumer is satisfied only when his expectations are delivered by the product. Understanding whether the consumers of a particular product category are satisfied or not, is very important to the marketers of the product. As a matter of fact, a consumer who is dissatisfied consumer shifts to the other brand and may influence others not to use the product. Following Table 82 presents the information gather in this aspect.

Table 82
Consumer's satisfaction / dissatisfaction with the brand of TV presently in use

	No. of Respondents District-wise						
Response Category	*Bishnupur*	*Thoubal*	*Imphal East*	*Imphal West*	*Church-andpur*	*Total*	*Per-centage*
c. Satisfied	145	110	110	133	43	541	89.71
d. Dissatisfied	17	9	11	15	10	62	10.28
Total	162	119	121	148	53	603	100

Its evident from the above table that majority of the respondents i.e. 89.71 % are satisfied with the TV they own. Dissatisfaction comes mainly from the respondents who have owned old model TV. Their dissatisfaction are related to poor picture quality, poor sound quality, problems associated with channel selection tuning and the lack of other features such as auto channel search, remote control etc.

11. *Brand Loyalty*

Some brands, due to the advertisement or the suggestion of the reference groups of the buyers, have an impact in the minds of the buyers. Buyers usually ask dealers for the brand of TV which they are familiar with. Moreover, some buyers are loyal to the brand of TV which they have already used and purchase the same brand in the second time purchase also.

Further, a brand loyal buyer when he does not get the brand of his choice in a particular shop, he goes to the other shop in search of the brand of his choice. In this regard, a question was put to the respondents. The responses gathered are presented in the Table 83.

Table 83

Step taken by the respondents when the brand of TV of their choice is not available in a particular shop

	No. of Respondents District-wise						
Response Category	*Bishnupur*	*Thoubal*	*Imphal East*	*Imphal West*	*Church-andpur*	*Total*	*Per-centage*
a. Ask for another brand of TV	74	35	55	46	9	219	36.31
b. Go to another shop to purchase the brand of his choice	88	84	66	102	44	384	63.68
Total	162	119	121	148	53	603	100

It is clear from the above table that 63.68% of the respondents go to another shop in search for the brand of TV of their choice whereas 36.31 % of the respondents ask for another brand of TV from the same shop when the brand of their choice is not available. This indicates that 63.68% of the respondents are brand loyal buyers. Further, it is found that in all the districts the numbers of brand loyal buyers are more than that of those who are not brand loyal.

12. ***Types of buying behaviour***

Depending upon the degree of consumers' involvement and the degree of perceived difference among the brands, consumers manifest different pattern of buying behaviour.

In order to access the types of buying behaviour that are associated with the purchase of TV, questions are put to the respondents in respect of the involvement of other members of the family and respondents perceived difference in the quality among the brands of TV available in the market. Responses so collected are computed in the following tables numbering 84 and 85.

Involvement of other members of the family

It is seen from the following Table that 81.92% of the respondents involve other members of the family in the purchase of a particular brand of TV whereas 18.07% of the respondents have the notion that there is no involvement of the other members of the family. It is also clear from the above table that in all the districts the number of respondents indicating the involvement of other members of the family is more than that of those who do not involve others.

Table 84

Involvement of other members of the family in the purchase decision of a particular brand of TV

	No. of Respondents District-wise						
Response Category	*Bishnupur*	*Thoubal*	*Imphal East*	*Imphal West*	*Church-andpur*	*Total*	*Per-centage*
a. Involvement	147	106	94	115	32	494	81.92
b. No involvement	15	13	27	33	21	109	18.07
Total	162	119	121	148	53	603	100

Buyer's perception of brand difference

Out of 603 respondents, 577 i.e. 95.68% of the respondents have perceived that there is significant difference among the available brands of TV. But, 4.31 % of the respondents feel that there is no significant difference among the available brands. The above description is based on the information presented in the Table 85.

Table 85
Buyer's perception of significant difference among the available brands of TV

Response Category	*No. of Respondents District-wise*						
	Bishnupur	*Thoubal*	*Imphal East*	*Imphal West*	*Church-andpur*	*Total*	*Per-centage*
a. Significant difference	158	113	118	140	48	577	95.68
b. No significant difference	4	6	3	8	5	26	4.31
Total	162	119	121	148	53	603	100

Types of buying behaviour

With a view to have a peep into the types of buying behaviour, further analysis is carried out. The analysis reveals that the number of respondents who indicate involvement and significant difference among the brands is 484. The number of respondents who indicate no involvement and significant difference among the brands is 93. Involvement and no significant difference are indicated by 10. And the number of respondents who indicate no involvement and no significant difference is 16.The above description is presented in the following Table 86.

Table 86
Involvement vis-à-vis brand difference

Degree of brand difference	*No. of respondents/Degree of involvement*		
	Involvement	*No involvement*	*Total*
Significant brand difference	484	93	577
No significant brand difference	10	16	26
Total	494	109	603

The above table depicts that 484 respondents out of 603 i.e. 80.26% of the respondents manifest complex buying behaviour. 10 respondents out of 603 i.e. 1.65% of the respondents exhibit dissonance reducing buying behaviour. Variety seeking buying behaviour is manifested by 93 i.e.15.42% of the respondents and habitual buying behaviour is associated with 16 i.e., 2.65% of the respondents.

5

Consumer Buying Decisions vis-a-vis Promotional Strategies and Reference Groups

Introduction

It is important for the business organisation to know what makes consumers to decide in their purchase decisions. Are consumers guided by logical reasoning and facts or taken away by sensory feelings? Answer to this will help marketer to develop appropriate promotional strategies to suit the consumer market.

Some consumers make rational decisions while other makes emotional decisions.

Rational decision-making implies that consumers are aware of the product alternatives, capable of correctly ranking each alternative in terms of benefits and disadvantages and able to identify the best alternatives.

An emotional decision-making means consumers make purchase decisions on impulse or on whim because they are emotionally driven rather than carefully searching and evaluating the information before buying. Here, consumers are basically submissive to the self-serving interest and promotional efforts of marketers. They yield to the aims and arms of marketers. Moreover, consumers' preference of a particular brand is also influenced by their reference groups. This chapter is an attempt to determine whether the consumers of Manipur make rational or emotional buying decisions. In this regard, for validating the hypothesis that

"The consumers of Manipur are falling prey to the strategies of the various marketing organisation as their buying decisions are far from sound and rational", following assumptions which govern the present study are subjected to test for each of the products chosen for the study. The assumptions are:

A. Consumers' brand preference is dependent on promotional strategies i.e., advertising, discount, and free gift offers of the company

B. Consumers' brand preference is dependent on its reference groups i.e., recommendation of friends, family, relatives and colleagues.

Testing of the Assumptions with Reference to the Buying of the Non-durable Goods (Toilet Soap)

The two assumptions given in A and B are separately tested by using the data collected from respondents in respect of toilet soap.

1. *Testing of the assumption a with reference to toilet soap*

For testing this assumption, respondents are served with a question in the questionnaire asking them to give the appropriate response as very important, or somewhat important, or not very important, or not at all important with respect to the statement "in your selection of a particular brand of toilet soap, how far advertising, discount and free gift offers are important." The responses that are collected from 752 respondents covering from 5 districts of Manipur are computed in the following table.

Table 87

Degree of importance of promotional strategies in the selection of brand of toilet soap

Response Category	*No of Respondents – Category-wise*					
	Bishnupur	*Thoubal*	*Imphal East*	*Imphal West*	*Churchand-pur*	*Total*
Very Important	67	65	29	32	29	222
Somewhat Important	67	63	80	88	40	338
Not Very Important	24	02	29	22	11	88
Not at all Important	15	21	13	37	18	104
Total	173	151	151	179	98	752

Consumers' brand preference in relation to promotional strategies

For understanding the degree of importance of promotional strategies in consumers' choice of a particular brand of toilet soap, Table 87 is reproduced as in Table 88.

Table 88

Worksheet for the calculation of average response of the degree of importance of promotional strategies (toilet soap)

Response category	*No. of respondents*	*Cumulative frequency*	*Median Response*
Very important	222	222	
Somewhatimportant			
Somewhat important	338	560	
Not very important	88	648	
Not at all important	104	752	

Note: Median = Size of {(n+ 1)/2}th item = Size of {(752 + 1)/2}th item = Size of 376. 5th item = somewhat important

The above table reveals that consumers' have the feeling of promotional strategies somewhat important in the selection of a particular brand of toilet soap.

Steps in the testing of the assumption A with reference to toilet soap:

Step 1. Null Hypothesis; there is no significant difference in the score among the various degree of importance.

Alternative hypothesis; there is significant difference in the score among the various degree of importance.

Step 2. Significant level á is taken at 5%

Step 3. Kolmogrov Smirnov D test is chosen because the data are ordinally scaled and one sampled data.

Step 4. Decision Rule

If the calculated value of D < table value of D, =>Null hypothesis is accepted

If the calculated value of D > Table Value of D, => Null hypothesis is rejected and Alternative hypothesis is accepted

Step 5. Calculation

Table 89

Work Sheet for the Kolmogrov Smirnov D for testing the significance of the importance of promotional strategies in buying decisions (toilet soap)

Response Category	*No. of Respondents*	*Observed Proportion*	*Observed Cum Proportion*	*Null Proportion*	*Null cum Proportion*	*Absolute difference between Observed and Null cum Proportion*	*Calculated value of D*
Very Important	222	.2952127	.2952127	.25	.25	.0452127	.24468
Somewhat Important	338	.449468	.7446807	.25	.50	.2446807	
Not Very Important	88	.1170212	.8617019	.25	.75	.1117019	
Not at all important	104	.1382978	.9999997	.25	1.00	.0000003	
Total	752						

Here, calculated value of D = Max | observed cum proportion - Null cum proportion |

D from the table is given by 1.36/√n; w here n is the sample size

Therefore, D = 1,36/√7 52 = 0.049594

Step 6 : Statistical Inference

Since, the calculated value of D (0.24468) > table value of D (0.049594)

=>Null hypothesis is rejected and Alternative hypothesis is accepted. i.e., there is significant difference in the score among the various degree of importance.

It is also observed that the number of respondents who consider the statement important is 560 (222 + 338) i.e., 74.46% of the respondents consider the statement important. Hence, consumers' brand preference is dependent on promotional strategies of the company.

2. ***Testing of the assumption B with reference to toilet soap***

For testing this assumption, respondents are served with a question in the questionnaire asking them to give appropriate response as strongly agree, or somewhat agree, or neutral, or somewhat disagree, or strongly disagree with respect to the statement.

"Recommendation of friends, family, relative and colleagues is very important in the selection of a particular brand of toilet soap."

The responses are computed in the following table.

Table 90
Degree of importance of the reference groups in the selection of a particular brand of toilet soap

Response Category	*No of Respondents – Category-wise*					
	Bishnupur	*Thoubal*	*Imphal East*	*Imphal West*	*Churchand-pur*	*Total*
Strongly agree	24	47	21	21	33	146
Somewhat agree	102	64	73	72	35	346
Neutral	39	33	46	80	11	209
Somewhat agree	6	3	5	5	9	28
Strongly disagree	2	4	6	1	10	23
Total	173	151	151	179	98	752

Consumers' brand preference in relation to reference groups

For describing the degree of importance of reference groups in consumers' selection of a particular brand of toilet soap, Table 90 reproduced as Table 91.

Table 91
Worksheet for the calculation of average response of the degree of importance of reference groups (toilet soap)

Response category	*No. of respondents*	*Cumulative frequency*	*Median response*
Strongly agree	146	146	
Somewhat agree	346	492	
Neutral	209	701	Somewhat agree
Somewhat disagree	28	729	
Strongly disagree	23	752	

Note: Median = Size of $\{(n+1)/2\}^{th}$ item = Size of $\{(752 + 1)/2\}^{th}$ item
= Size of 376. 5th item = somewhat agree

The above table depicts that the consumers are of the opinion that reference groups are somewhat very important in the selection of a particular brand of toilet soap.

Steps in the testing of the assumption B with reference to toilet soap

Step 1. Null hypothesis; there is no significant difference in the score among the various degree of agreement.

Alternative hypothesis; there is significant difference in the score among the various degree of agreement,

Step 2. Significant level á is taken at 5%.

Step 3. Kolmogrov Smirnov D test is chosen because the data are ordinally scaled and one sampled data

Step 4. Decision rule;

If the calculated value of D<table table of D

=>Null hypothesis is accepted

If the calculated value of D > table value of D

=> Null hypothesis is rejected Alternative hypothesis is accepted.

Step 5 : Calcu!ation

Table 92

Worksheet for the Kolmogrov Smirnov D for testing the significance of the importance of reference groups (toilet soap)

Response Category	*No. of Respondents*	*Observed Proportion*	*Observed Cum Proportion*	*Null Proportion*	*Null cum Proportion*	*Absolute difference between Observed and Null cum Proportion*	*Calculated value of D*
Strongly agree	146	.1941489	.194189	.20	.20	.00581	.3321
Somewhat agree	346	.4601063	.6542552	.20	.40	.25425	
Neutral	209	.2779255	.93241807	.20	.60	.33218	
Somewhat agree	28	.037234	.9694147	.20	.80	.16941	
Strongly disagree	23	.0305851	.9999998	.20	1	.0000002	
Total	752						

Here, calculated value of D = Max I observed cum proportion - Null cum proportion I

D from the table is given by $1.36/\sqrt{n}$

Therefore, $D = 1.36/\sqrt{752}$

$= 0.04959$

Step 6 : Statistical Inference

Since, the calculated value of D (0.3321) > table value of D(0.04959)

=> Null hypothesis is rejected and Alternative hypothesis is accepted.i.e. there is significant difference in the score among the various degree of agreement. Moreover, it is also observed that the number of respondents who consider the statement important is 492 (146 + 346) i.e., 65.42% of the respondents Agree to the statement.

Hence, consumers' brand preference is dependent on its reference groups.

Testing of the Assumptions with Reference to the Buying of Durable Goods (TV)

The two assumptions given in A and B are separately tested by using the data collected from respondents in respect of T.V.

1. *Testing of the assumption A with reference to TV*

Out of the 752 households covered, there are 603 who own TV set. For testing the assumption A, a question is served in the questionnaire to 603 respondents who own TV set requesting them to tick an appropriate response i.e. very important, or somewhat important, or not very important, or not at all important with respect to the statement

"In your selection of a particular brand of TV set, how far advertising, discount, free gift offers are important."

The responses so collected are computed as given below.

Table 93
Degree of importance of promotional strategies in the selection of brand of TV

Response Category	*No of Respondents – Category-wise*					
	Bishnupur	*Thoubal*	*Imphal East*	*Imphal West*	*Churchand-pur*	*Total*
Very Important	53	54	54	17	16	194
Somewhat Important	90	50	55	96	20	311
Not Very Important	9	1	7	14	6	37
Not at all Important	10	14	5	21	11	61
Total	162	119	121	148	53	603

Consumers' brand preference in relation to promotional strategies

For portraying the degree of importance of promotional strategies in the selection of a particular brand of TV, Table 93 is reproduced as Table 94.

Table 94
Worksheet for the calculation of average response of the degree of importance of promotional strategies (TV).

Response category	*No. of respondents*	*Cumulative frequency*	*Median response*
Very important	194	194	
Somewhat important	311	505	Somewhat important
Not very important	37	542	
Not at all important	61	603	

Note: Median = Size of $\{(n+1)/2\}^{th}$ item = Size of $\{(603+1)/2\}^{th}$ item
= Size of 302 th item = somewhat important

It is seen from the above table that consumers have the notion that promotional strategies are somewhat important in the selection of a particular brand of TV.

Steps in the testing of assumption A with reference to T.V

Step 1. Null Hypothesis; there is no significant difference in the score among the various degree of importance.

Alternative hypothesis; there is significant difference in the score among the various degree of importance.

Step 2. Significant level á is taken at 5%

Step 3. Kolmogrov Smirnov D test is chosen because the data are ordinally scaled and one sampled data.

Step 4. Decision Rule.

If the calculated value of D < table value of D

==>Null hypothesis is accepted

If the calculated value of D > Table Value of D

=>Null hypothesis is rejected and Alternative hypothesis is accepted

Step 5. Calculation

Table 95

Work Sheet for the Kolmogrov Smirnov D for testing the significance of the importance of promotional strategies in buying decisions(TV)

Response Category	*No. of Respondents*	*Observed Proportion*	*Observed Cum Proportion*	*Null Proportion*	*Null cum Proportion*	*Absolute difference between Observed and Null cum Proportion*	*Calculated value of D*
Very Important	194	.03217247	.3217247	.25	.25	.0717247	.33747
Somewhat Important	311	.5157545	.8374792	.25	.50	.3374792	
Not Very Important	37	.0613598	.898839	.25	.75	.148839	
Not at all Important	61	.1011608	.9999998	.25	1.00	.0000002	
Total	603						

Here, calculated value of D = Max | observed cum proportion - Null cum proportion |

D from the table is given by $1.36/\sqrt{n}$.

Therefore, $D = 1.36/\sqrt{603}$

$=0.05538$

Step 6 : Statistical Inference

Since, the calculated value of D (0.33747) > table value of D (0.05538)

=>Null hypothesis is rejected and the Alternative hypothesis is accepted.

i.e. there is significant difference in the score among the various degree of agreement. Moreover, it is also observed that the number of respondents who consider the statement important is 505 (194 + 311) i.e. 83.74% of the respondents consider that promotional strategies of the company are important in the selection of a particular brand of TV.

Hence, consumers' brand preference of TV is dependent on promotional strategies.

2. ***Testing of the assumption B with reference to TV***

For testing this assumption, 603 respondents who own TV set are served a question in the questionnaire requesting them to tick a response that suits their opinion as strongly agree, or somewhat agree, or neutral, or somewhat disagree, or strongly disagree with respect to the statement

"Recommendation of friends, family, relative and colleagues is very important in the selection of a particular brand of TV set".

The responses so collected from these 603 respondents are computed against the various response categories as given below.

Table 96
Degree of importance of the reference groups in the selection of a particular brand of TV

Response Category	*No of Respondents – Category-wise*					
	Bishnupur	*Thoubal*	*Impahl East*	*Imphal West*	*Churchand-pur*	*Total*
Strongly agree	30	37	34	17	17	135
Somewhat agree	96	50	51	70	21	288
Neutral	32	30	32	59	4	157
Somewhat agree	1	1	1	2	3	8
Strongly disagree	3	1	3	0	8	15
Total	162	119	121	148	53	603

Consumers' brand preference in relation to reference group

For describing the degree of importance of reference group in the selection of a particular brand of TV, Table 96 is reproduced as in Table 97.

Table 97
Worksheet for the calculation of average response of the degree of importance of reference groups (TV)

Response category	*No. of Respondents*	*Cumulative frequency*	*Median response*
Strongly agree	135	135	Somewhat agree
Somewhat agree	288	423	
Neutral	157	580	
Somewhat disagree	8	588	
Strongly disagree	15	603	

Note: Median = Size of {(n+ 1)/2}th item = Size of {(603+ 1)}th item
= Size of 302nd item = somewhat agree

The above table depicts that consumers have the feeling that reference groups are somewhat very important in the selection of a particular brand of TV.

Steps in the testing of the assumption B with reference to TV

Step 1. Null hypothesis; there is no significant difference in the score among the various degree of agreement.

Alternative hypothesis; there is significant difference in the score among the various degree of agreement.

Step: 2. significant level á is taken at 5%.

Step: 3. Kolmogrov Smirnov D test is chosen because the data are ordinally scaled and one sampled data.

Step: 4. Decision rule;

If the calculated value of D<table value of D

=>Null hypothesis is accepted

If the calculated value of D > table value of D

=>Null hypothesis is rejected and Alternative hypothesis is accepted

Step: 5. Calculation.

Table 98
Worksheet for the Kolmogrov Smirnov D for testing the significance of the importance of reference groups (TV)

Response Category	*No. of Respondents*	*Observed Proportion*	*Observed Cum Proportion*	*Null Proportion*	*Null cum Proportion*	*Absolute difference between Observed and Null cum Proportion*	*Calculated value of D*
Strongly agree	135	.2238806	.2238806	.2	.2	.0238806	.3618
Somewhat agree	288	.4776119	.7014925	.2	.4	.3014925	
Neutral	157	.2603648	.9618573	.2	.6	.3618573	
Somewhat agree	8	.0132669	.9751242	.2	.8	.1751242	
Strongly disagree	15	.0248756	.9999998	.2	1	.0000002	
Total	603						

Here, calculated value of D = Max | observed cum proportion - Null cum proportion |

D from the table is given by $1.36/\sqrt{n}$

Therefore, $D = 1.36/\sqrt{603}$
Therefore, D = 0.0553834

Step: 6. Statistical Inference

Since, the calculated value of D (0.3618573) > table value of D (0.0553834)

=>Null hypothesis is rejected and Alternative hypothesis is accepted.

i.e., there is significant difference in the score among the various degree of agreement. Moreover, it is observed that the number of respondents who consider the statement important is 423 (135 + 288) i.e., 70.14% of the respondents Agree to the statement. Hence, consumer's brand preference is dependent on its reference groups.

Validation of Hypothesis of the Study

From the above testing of the assumptions with reference to both the consumer non-durable goods (toilet soap) and the durable goods (TV), it can be concluded that

i). Consumers' brand preference is dependent on promotional strategies i.e. advertising, discount and free gift offers of the company.

ii). Consumers' brand preference is dependent on its reference groups i.e. recommendation of friends, family, relatives and colleagues.

Hence, the hypothesis of the present study, that is "the consumer of Manipur are falling prey to the strategies of the various marketing organisations as their buying decisions are far from sound and rational" is validated.

In other words, the consumers of Manipur are passive and emotional in their buying decisions.

6

Marketing Strategy Development for Non-Durable Goods (Toilet Soap) and Durable Goods (TV) Markets of Manipur

Introduction

India, after liberalising her economy, has benefited in many fields. It has improved the efficiency of the Industry. It has also enabled the domestic industries to reach to the international market.

As a result of the changes taking place in the economy, Indian domestic markets of consumer durable and non-durable goods are also growing rapidly.

For the consumers, the changes have been heralded by a very large number of foreign brands now available legally on shop shelves. The competition is fierce and the consumers have benefited not just by price slashes but deferred payment, home deliveries, gifts and extended free service.

However, the impact of liberalisation in the form of brand proliferation in Manipur consumer market and subsequent benefit to the consumer is not felt to the expectation. A deep look into the consumer markets of durable and non-durable goods reveals that Manipur Market deserves to be given attention by the marketer, for it is a growing market the potential of which is yet to be fully tapped.

Manipur is a small state situated in the North Eastern corner of India bordering Myanmar (Burma). It lies between 23.53° N and 25.41°N latitude and longitude 93.2°E and 94.47°E. The geographical area of Manipur is only 22,327 sq. km. Its neighbouring states are Nagaland on the North, Assam on the West and Mizoram on the South and Southwest.

As per the 2001 census, Manipur has a population of 2,388634 persons consisting of 1207,338 males and 1181296 female. The child population in the age group 0-6 is 13.09% of the total population. The literacy rate is 68.87% comprising 77.87% of males and 59.70% females.

The estimated number of households of Manipur is 399437. Majority of the people of Manipur are Hindu. The composition of religion of the people as per the 1991 census is given below.

Religion	*Percentage of population*
Hindu	57.66
Sikh	0.07
Muslim	7.26
Christian	34.11
Jain	0.07
Buddhist	0.03
Others	0.76
Total	100

The estimated average size of the family in Manipur is 6 persons. An on 30.6.2000, there are 63,829 state govt. employees, 3305 quasi-government employees and 3651 local body employees. About two-third of the main workers in Manipur are engaged in Agriculture as cultivators and agriculture labourers. Further, the decadal growth rate of the population is 30.02%. In 2001, the population of Manipur is 0.23% of the total of all India.

In Manipur, there are not many large scale industries. Handloom weaving is the largest single cottage industry. Other cottage industries are sericulture, bamboo and cane articles, carpentry, blacksmith, leather goods, edible oil crushing, rice milling, gur and khandsari.

Manipur Electronics Development Corporation Ltd. (Manitron), a Govt. of Manipur undertaking assembles and markets Manitron brand of TV sets. But for the last several months this corporation is not doing any business activity. The people of Manipur for its household consumption or use of many non-durable goods such as toilet soap, tooth paste, shampoo, etc and durable goods such as TV, refrigerator, washing machine, etc. depend on the products which are manufactured outside the state.

So, Manipur with its decadal growth rate of population of 30.02% which is higher than 21.34% of all India is a growing market and the knowledge of which will be of immense help to the marketers of non-durable and durable goods in Manipur for formulating appropriate marketing strategies for the satisfaction of consumers and profit to the company.

Moreover, market trend and consumer behaviour of many non-durable goods are similar and it is also the same case with the durable goods. So by understanding consumer market and consumer behaviour of a product in non-durable or durable category, one can infer to some extent the characteristics of other products in the same category.

Consumer Non-durable Goods (Toilet Soap) Market of Manipur

Available and use brands

In all there are about 38 brands of toilet soap which are available in Manipur in different varieties, sizes and MRPs (Table 1). The majority of the households i.e. 62.89% use single brand. And about 20.7% of the households use two, 9.97% use three and 7.04% use four brands of toilet soap (Table 2).

Usage rate

The daily average usage rate of a person is three times. The usage rate of female is slightly higher than that of a male (Table 5 and 6). Majority of the consumers i.e. 76.72% use a particular brand of toilet soap for one or more years which is an indicative of the tendency of the consumers becoming brand loyal consumers (Table 9).

Market share of toilet soaps

Share of volume and market value of consumption

Beauty brand of toilet soap occupies the highest share of volume of consumption accounting for 14.90% followed by Cinthol and Lux brands with 13.54% and 11.63% respectively (Table 11).

But the highest share of market value of consumption is occupied by Cinthol with 14.35% followed by Lux and Beauty brands with 12.70% and 11.84% respectively. Beauty brand in spite of having the highest share of volume of consumption has occupied third place in the market value of consumption because of its economical pricing (Table 12). Beauty brand of toilet soap is purchased mainly because of its economic price by the consumers of low income segment. Cinthol and Lux brands are purchased mainly by the consumers of middle income segment because of their brand image, attractive packaging, and availability of wide range of variety.

Size segment

On the size segment, 75 gm packet occupies the highest share of number of pieces purchase as well as market value of consumption with 47.87% and 45.18% respectively. The second place is occupied by size 100 gm with 38.11 % of share of number pieces purchase and the market value of 42.96% (Table 13).

Price segment

In price segment, the price range "Rs.8 and less than Rs.12" has the largest share of pieces of toilet soap purchase with 47.5% and the highest market value with 38.38%.The second place is occupied by the price range "Rs.12 but less than Rs.16" having 20.13% pieces of consumption and 22.79% of value of consumption (Table 14).

Per capita consumption

A person's monthly average consumption of pieces, volume of consumption and expenditure on toilet soap are one piece, 84.16 gm and Rs.12.50 (approximately) respectively (Table 15).

Per capita consumption of toilet soap in Manipur is 1.009 kg where as that of India is 0.70 kg (Table 19).

Per capita consumption of some Asian countries is given below:

Table 99
Per capita consumption of toilet soap in some Asian countries

Country	*Per capita consumption (1994) Kg*
Taiwan	6.2
Thailand	3.2
Indonesia	2.0
Korea	3.3
Malaysia	3.7
Japan	8.9

Source: Majumdar, Ramanuj, *Product Management in India,* 2nd edition Prentice Hall of India, New Delhi, 2000. p. 171.

The difference in the per capita consumption of toilet soap is mainly due to the difference in the washing habits of the people.

Share of Manipur in the Indian domestic consumption in the year 2001

The Estimated consumption of toilet soap in Manipur for the year 2001 is 2.412324 thousand tonnes and that of all Indian domestic consumption is 727.13 thousand tonnes. Therefore, the share of Manipur toilet soap market by volume in the Indian domestic market is 0.33% (Table 18 and 20).

Further, the estimated market value of consumption in Manipur is Rs.35.8581732 crores and that of all India is Rs. 10457.7 crores. Therefore, the share of Manipur toilet soap market by value in the Indian domestic market is 0.34% (Table 22 and 23).

Consumer Durable Goods (TV) Market of Manipur

Brand ownership of the penetrated market

Till March 2002, 71.73% of households of Manipur have owned TV set(s) out of the total estimated households of 3,99,437. The percentage of TV ownership in the valley districts of Manipur is higher than that of hill Districts. In the valley district, it is 84.09% whereas in the hill districts it is 54.08% (Table 24 and 25).

Among the TV owners, 78.27% have single TV set, where as 20.23% and 14.9% have two and three TV sets respectively. Ownership by type of TV is concerned, 62.52% have a single colour TV set whereas15.75% have a single black and white TV set. Further, 10.28% of the TV owners have two TV sets in which one is black and white and the other is colour (Table 26).

Preferred brands by the present non owners of TV

Among all the TV Brands which the people who do not

presently own TV set would like to buy is Sony which accounts for 22.14% followed by Philips and Onida with 14.76% and 8.72% respectively (Table 27).

Colour TV segments of the penetrated market

There are about 35 brands of TV which have penetrated the households of Manipur. Of all the brands, Onida constitutes the highest share with 15.13% followed by Sony and Video con brands with 14.08%and 13.21 % respectively (Table 28).

Size segment

Of all sizes, 21 inch model constitutes the highest share accounting for 84.52%. This is followed by 14 inch model with 7.65 % (Table 30).

Annual average growth rate

The Annual average growth rate of colour TV market by piece purchase during the period 1995 - 2001 is 14.08% and Annual average growth rate of market value during the same period is 14.87%.

Black and White TV segment of the penetrated market

There are about 30 black and white TV brands that have penetrated the households of Manipur. Of all the brands, Onida constitutes the highest share with 19.39% followed by Phillips and Manitron with18.78% and 9.09% respectively (Table 29).

Size segment

The most popular size is 14 inch model accounting for 84,24% and the second place is occupied by 21 inch model which accounts for 13.93% (Table 30).

Annual average growth rate

The annual average growth rate of black and white TV

market by pieces purchase during the period 1995 -2001 is (-) 13.76% i.e. black and white TV market is declining at the rate of 13.76%. During the same period, value of the market is also declining at the rate of 20.93%. Due to the declining in the sales of black and white TV purchase, dealers are not planning to stock black and white TV in the near future.

Sales of TV in the year 2001 in Manipur

In all there are 7 main dealers of TV selling of different brands. TV brands available in the market are LG, Videocon, Philips, Onida, Thomson, Sony, Samsung, BPL and Akai.

Among all the brands, Akai has the highest share of market value accounting for 31.19% followed by L.G. and Videocon with 30.45% and 13.01 % respectively (Table 36). In the mind of today's buyers of TV in Manipur, Akai and LG brands are associated with hi-fi system, new technology, popular, quality product and foreign brand. It is because of this reason, sales of these brands are high in Manipur.

Size segment

Of all the sizes available (i.e, 14 inches, 17 inches, 20 inches,21 inches, 29 inches and 34 inches), 21 inches model constitutes the highest share with 44.87%. This model is followed by 14 inches and 20 inches with 23.96% and 14.85% respectively. (Table 38).

Price segment

In the price segment, the price range "Rs. 1 0,000/- but less than Rs. 15,000/-"constitutes the highest share of market value accounting for 34.37%. This is followed by the price range "below Rs. 10,000/-"and "Rs. 15,000/- but less than Rs. 20,000/-"with 24.35% and 18.44% respectively. (Table 39).

Value of the market

The estimated total sales of TV set in Manipur in the

year 2001 is 9384 pieces and the value of the market is Rs. 12.0388260 crores.(Table 37).

Share of Manipur TV market in the Indian domestic market in the year 2001

The estimated purchase of TV sets in Indian domestic market in the year 2001 is 7866000 units. (Table 41).Therefore, the share of TV sets sold in Manipur in the Indian domestic market of TV is 0.119% (Table 42).

Further, the estimated value of TV market in the Indian domestic market for the same year is Rs. 7195.67 crores. Thus, the share of Manipur market value of TV in the Indian domestic market in the year2001 is 0.167% (Table 45).

Consumer Buying Behaviour of Non-durable Goods (Toilet Soap) and Durable Goods (TV) in Manipur

1. ***Consumer's background***

The consumer behaviour that is the things they buy is influenced by consumer's background i.e., culture, personality and social class.

Culture

The percentage composition and the culture which the consumers of Manipur belong to are health or fitness (21.67%), achievement (20.74%), positive (16.35%), independent (15.29%), social or interactive (14.36%) and materialistic (11.56%). (Table 46).

Personality

About 45.61 % of the consumers of Manipur belong to the detached personality while 27.79% and 26.59% belong to Compliant and Aggressive Cultures respectively. (Table 47).

Social class

A large number of consumers (i.e., 77.79%) consider

themselves belonging to middle class. About 15.29% belong to lower class and a small percentage of 6.9% belongs to the upper class. (Table 48).

2. ***Consumer buying behaviour of non-durable goods (toilet soap)***

Awareness level of different brands of toilet soap

Of all the brands of toilet soap, Lux has cent percent awareness among the consumers of Manipur. Lifebuoy, Cinthol and Beauty occupy the second, third and fourth places respectively in the level of awareness. (Table 49)

Preferable (use) brand of toilet soap

Majority of the consumers i.e., 15.15% use Cinthol brand. This is followed by Lux, Beauty, and Lifebuoy with 13.03%, 12.36% and 9.57% respectively.

Users

In 75.93% of the households, a particular brand of toilet soap which is used by a consumer is also used by any members of the family (Table 59)

It can also be mentioned here that 62.89% of the households use single brand of toilet soap (Table 2).

Outlets of purchase

A large number of consumers frequently buy their toilet soap from nearby general stores. This constitutes 47.60%. And 24.10%, 13.56%and 11.17% of respondents purchase their toilet soap frequently from main market general stores, main market cosmetic store and nearby Pan Dukan respectively (Table 61).

Purchase amount

Majority of the consumers (31.78%) purchase only one pieces of toilet soap at a time while two and three pieces are purchased by17.42% and 17.28% of the consumers respectively. (Table 62). Other important aspects of consumer behaviour are discussed in the comparative study of non durable goods (toilet soap) and durable goods (TV) in a paragraph to follow.

3. *Consumer buying behaviour of durable goods (TV)*

Awareness level of different brands of TV

Of all the brands of TV, Onida, Philips and Manitron have the cent percent awareness level among the consumers of Manipur. Sony and Videocon occupy the second and third highest awareness level with 93.75% and 92.05% respectively (Table 68).

Preferable (use) brands of TV

Among all the brands, Onida is the brand which is preferred and used by most of the consumers. Onida is used by 15.92% of the TV owners. Sony occupies the second place with 12.93%. Philips and Videocon occupy the third place with 12.10% each. (Table 78).

Mode of purchase

Purchase of TV by cash constitutes highest share with 54.39%.This is followed by easy instalment scheme given by dealers with 21.72%.The third place is occupied by Marup (local scheme) with 11.94% (Table 80).

Outlets of purchase

Majority of the consumers i.e., 69.65% purchase their TV from state capital whereas 24.04% purchase from the local dealers or agency and a small number of people (6.3%) purchases from outside the state. (Table 79)

Purchase occasions

Majority of the consumers (48.59%) purchase their TV

on occasions such as when the family financial position is sound, New Year, birthday, any family occasions and when the family felt the necessity of having a TV set. This is followed by major international/national sports events (25.53%) and marriage gift (23.38%). (Table 81).

4. *A comparative study of consumer buying behaviour of non-durable goods (toilet soap) and durable goods (TV) in some important aspects of consumer behaviour*

This portion of the present chapter tries to portray a comparative picture of the buying behaviour between non-durable goods (toilet soap) and durable goods (TV) for easy grasping of the degree of similarity or dissimilarity between the two.

The following table presents in brief a comparative picture of non-durable goods and durable goods in some important aspects of consumer buying behaviour.

Table 100
A comparative study of consumer buying behaviour between non-durable goods (toilet soap) and durable goods (TV)

Aspects of consumer behaviour	*Features of the aspects considered*	
	Non-durable goods (toilet soap)	*Durable goods (TV)*
1	*2*	*3*
1. Two important sources of information	Public sources (39.76%) personal sources (28.85%)	Public sources (52.07%) Personal sources (30.01)
2. Three important product factor (benefit sought)	Freshness/deodorant, health /germ protection and skin care	Picture quality, sound quality and durability

(Contd....)

1	2	3
3. Three Important Marketing Factor	Product benefits, advertising and recommendation of retailers	Product benefits, advertising and warranty
4. Buying Roles		
i. Two Important initiators	Youngsters (37.23%) and Mother (30.58%)	Mother (33.33%) and Youngsters (26.53)
ii. Two important influencers	Neighbours/relatives friends (54.65) and co-workers colleagues (21.8%)	Neighbours/relatives friends (44.11%) and co-workers colleagues (34.66%)
iii. Two important deciders	Mother (33.24%) and Youngsters (28.05%)	Father (40.29%) and mother (27.52%)
iv. Two important buyers	Any member of the family (36.96%) and mother (28.05%)	Father (59.63%) and youngsters (15.09%)
5. Percentage of satisfied consumers	95.4% of respondents	89.71% of respondents (TV owners)
6. Percentage of Brand loyal consumers	54.64% of respondents	63.68% of respondents (TV owners)
7. Types of buying behaviour of the majority of the consumers	73% exhibit complex buying behaviour	80.26% exhibit complex buying behaviour

Note: Percentages given in the parentheses for non-durable goods (toilet soap) are calculated from the total respondents of 752 whereas in the case of durable goods they are calculated from the total of 603 respondents (TV owners).

Two important sources of information (Table 50, Table 69 and Table 100)

The two important sources of information from which consumers come to know about the non-durable goods (toilet soap) and durable goods (TV) are public sources and personal sources. Public sources consist of TV, radio, newspapers and magazines whereas personal sources comprise family, friends and neighbours. It is also observed that the degree of utilisation of these sources in the consumer purchase decision is more in the case of durable goods (TV) than that of non-durable goods (toilet soap).

Three important product factors (benefits sought) Table 51, Table 70and Table 100)

Three important benefits sought by the consumers in the purchase decision of toilet soap are freshness/deodorant, health/germ protection and skincare whereas the three important benefits sought by the consumers of TV are picture quality, sound quality, and durability.

Three important marketing factors (Table 53, table 72, and Table 100)

Three important marketing factors or strategies to which the consumers of toilet soap have positive response are product benefits, recommendation of retailers. And the three important marketing factors in the case of TV are product benefits, advertising and warranty.

Buying roles

People play different roles in buying decision. They may be initiators, influencers, deciders and buyers

i) *Two important initiators (Table 55, Table 74 and table 100)*

   Two important initiators in both the cases of toilet soap and TV are youngsters and mother in the family. But, youngsters are the main initiators in the case of toilet soap whereas the main initiator in the case of TV is mother.

ii) *Two important influencers (Table 56, Table 75 and Table 100)*

   For the two product categories, neighbours/relative/ friends and co-workers/colleague are the two important influencers. But neighbours/ relatives/

friends have relatively higher degree of influence on the consumers in the case of toilet soap than that of TV.

iii) *Two important deciders (Table 57, Table 76 and Table 100)*

Two important deciders in the choice of a particular brand of toilet soap are mother and youngsters in the family whereas father and mother are the deciders in the case of TV. But the main decider in the case of toilet soap is mother whereas father is the main decider in the case of TV.

iv) *Two important buyers (Table 58, Table 77, and table 100)*

Two important buyers of toilet soap are any members of the family and mother. And the two important buyers of TV are father and youngsters. It is also observed that the main buyers of toilet soap are any members of the family whereas the main buyers of TV are father.

Percentage of satisfied consumers (Table 63, Table 82 and Table 100)

The percentage of respondents who are satisfied with the brand of toilet soap which they are using is 95.4%. The dissatisfaction of the consumers includes high price, non durability of soap and frequent non-availability of a particular brand of choice. And the percentage of respondents (TV owners) who are satisfied with the brands of TV they are owning are 89.71 %. Dissatisfaction comes mainly from the respondents who owned old TV models and their dissatisfaction is related with poor sound quality, poor picture quality and the lack of other features such as remote control, auto channel selection, etc.

Percentage of brand loyal consumers (Table 64, Table 83 and Table 100)

Percentages of brand loyal consumers of toilet soap and

percentage of brand loyal owners of TV are 54.64% and 63.68% respectively. This indicates that consumers are more brand loyal in the case of durable goods than that of non-durable goods.

Types of buying behaviour of the majority of consumers (Table 67, Table 86 and Table 100)

In the case of toilet soap, the percentage of respondents that exhibits complex buying behaviour is 73%. But 80.26% of respondents who owned TV manifest complex buying behaviour. From this finding it can be inferred that buying durable goods (TV) exhibits higher degree of complex buying behaviour than that of non-durable goods (toilet soap).

Appropriate Marketing Strategy for the Consumer Non-durable Goods (Toilet Soap) and Durable Goods (TV) Markets of Manipur

According to Kotler, marketing strategy comprises the broad principles by which marketing management expects to achieve its business and marketing objectives in a target market. It consists of basic decisions on marketing expenditure, marketing mix and marketing allocation. The marketing mix to be taken up by the marketer is discussed in four factors i.e. product, price, place and promotion. These four factors have been popularised by McCarthy as four Ps. Philip Kotler defines the term marketer as someone seeking a response from another party, called the prospect.

Here, for the purpose of the discussion, marketer refers to the business organisation or manager marketing non-durable goods (toilet soap) and durable goods (TV) in Manipur. And the prospects are the Manipur consumers of toilet soap and TV.

In the light of the findings of the study on consumer market and consumer behaviour of Manipur, appropriate marketing strategy suitable for Manipur consumer markets is discussed in the following paragraphs.

1. ***Marketing strategy for non-durable goods (toilet soap).***

Product decision

In product decision, only the aspects of the size and product variety which are relevant to the study are discussed here.

The marketer marketing toilet soap in Manipur should ensure that the product is made available in different sizes in the following proportion which is deduced from the number of size-wise pieces consumed by the consumers of Manipur (Table 13).

Table 101
Size-wise proportion of toilet soap to be to be marketed in Manipur

Size(gm)	*Proportion of toilet soap pieces*
50	0.013
70	0.0016
75	0.4787
80	0.068
90	0.0282
100	0.3811
125	0.0119
150	0.0171
Total	1

If the 85.98% of the toilet soap pieces produced are in 75 gm and 100 gm., then it will be a profitable proposition for the business organization as the maximum number of consumers of Manipur usually purchase in these two sizes under normal circumstances without the influence of any promotional activities.

Variety

The appropriate variety of toilet soap for the consumer market of Manipur should be related with freshness/ deodorant, health/germ protection and skin care because these are the three main benefits sought by the consumers of Manipur. (Table 51).

Product benefits mentioned above are also some of the important marketing factors, which produce positive response from the customers in the purchase of toilet soap. (Table 53).

As a matter of fact, these product benefits should be highlighted in the advertisement of the product.

Price decision

Depending upon the socio-economic condition and lifestyle, majority of the consumers purchase toilet soap at different price ranges. The ranges of MRP at which the toilet soap can be marketed and the proportions of the product to be manufactured for each price range are given below

Table 102

Price range and the proportion of toilet soap of each price range to be marketed in Manipur

Price range	*Proportion*
Rs. 8/- but less than Rs. 12/-	0.1585
Rs. 12/- but less than Rs. 16/-	0.4751
Rs. 16/- but less than Rs. 20/-	0.2013
Rs. 20/- but less than Rs. 25/-	0.1180
Rs. 25/- and above	0.0465
Total	01.000

The proportion given in the above table is derived from the information regarding the number of pieces sold against each price range (Table 14).

Place decision

In the marketing of fast moving consumer goods, what is important to the marketer is the maximum coverage of the available retail outlets. It is also mentioned in the chapter 4 that one of the dissatisfaction of the consumer regarding the toilet soap is the non-availability of the toilet soap as and when needed by them. Under the normal situation when various means are not used to influence consumers to purchase from a particular retail outlet, the following table presents the proportion of toilet soaps to be catered outlet-wise by the marketers for setting targets for retail coverage.

Table 103
Proportion of toilet soap to be catered outlet wise in Manipur

Nearby general stores	0.476
Main market general stores	0.2406
Nearby pan duke	0.1117
Main market cosmetic store	0.1356
Any others	0.057
Total	1.000

The proportion given in the above table is deduced from the number of consumers who frequently purchase their toilet soap from a particular outlet. (Table 61) As a matter of fact, if the company make their toilet soap available in as many as general stores, pan dukan and cosmetic store, more sales can be generated.

Promotion decision

Advertisement and sales promotion play very important role in the consumer's purchase decision of toilet soap in Manipur.

Advertisement is paid form of non-personal presentation and promotion of ideas, goods or services by an identified sponsor.

And the sales promotion is a short-term incentive to encourage purchase or sales of a product or services.

In chapter 5, it is already discussed that buyer's brand preference is dependent on promotional strategies (i.e., advertisement, discount and free gift offers) of the company and reference groups (i.e., recommendation of friends, family, relatives and colleagues).

In Table 2, it is highlighted that 62.89% of the households use only one brand of toilet soap which is an indicative of a family-oriented product.

In the purchase decision of toilet soap, main influencers are neighbours/relatives and co-workers and colleagues (Table 56).

The Table 65 reveals that in 75.39% of the households, there is involvement of other members of the family in the choice of a particular brand of toilet soap.

In the Table 55 and 57, it is depicted that the main initiators and deciders in the choice of a particular brand of toilet soap are youngsters (age between 15 and 25 years) and mother in the family.

And in the Table 58, it is revealed that the main buyers are any members of the family and mother.

In the Table 53, it is presented that the main marketing factors which enable to generate positive response from the consumers are product benefits, advertisement and recommendation of retailers.

It is also indicated in the Table 50 that the main sources of information of consumers in making purchase decision of toilet soap are TV, radio, newspaper and magazines.

With the help of the above information, appropriate advertising and sales promotional strategies for Manipur consumer market of toilet soap are discussed below.

Advertising

Budget for advertisement can be decided by the marketer depending upon the financial position of the company. Objectives of advertisement should be to create the awareness of the brand as well as to educate the consumers about the product (toilet soap). Message of the advertisement should highlight the product benefits i.e., freshness, germ protection and skin care.

The illustration component of the advertisement copy (for print Ad) and the picturisation for advertisement in TV should centre around either family or social environment. This is due to the fact that the purchase decision of toilet soap in Manipur involves other members of the family and the brand preference is dependent on their reference groups. The message should be desirable, exclusive and believable to the consumers of Manipur. Marketer should use emotional positioning approach (emotional appeal) as the toilet soap buyers of Manipur are passive and emotional. (Chapter 5).

The message should be targeted to the initiators, deciders and buyers of a brand of toilet soap.

Media vehicles

Depending upon the media habits of the consumers of Manipur, following media are the appropriate vehicles for advertisement. (Appendix V- media habits of consumers of Manipur).

Local newspaper (household)	*Share of readership (household)*	*Reach*
i) Sangai express	34.62%	35.77%
ii) Poknapham	34.36%	35.0%
Local magazine		
i) Athouba	25.31 %	5.31%
ii) Sanathong	46.83%	9.84%
National newspaper		
i) Telegraph	48.17%	26.32%
ii) Times of India	31.87%	17.42%
National magazine		
i) India Today	29.24%	13.96%.
ii) Outlook	14.20%	6.78%

For the TV Ad either in cable or Doordarshan, the appropriate timing for scheduling advertisement is in the evening when majority of the consumers watch TV programmes. To be precise, the timing of 6-9 p.m. is more appropriate for the consumers of Manipur because after 9 p.m, majority of the people go to sleep.

The effectiveness of the advertisement can be measured for (i) effectiveness of communication in terms of awareness through portfolio test (ii) effectiveness in terms of generating sales through sales effective research using experimental design of measuring sales before advertisement and after the advertisement.

Sales promotion

As recommendation of the retailers counts a lot in the purchase decision of toilet soap, higher margins or incentives should be given occasionally to the retailers. For the consumers of Manipur, schemes like 2+ 1 or 3+ 1 means a lot to them than that of any discount or the price reduction particularly in the case of toilet soap.

2. *Marketing strategy for durable goods (TV)*

Product decision

Analysis of the purchase of TV in Manipur reveals that different people opted for different sizes. The product sorting of the sizes of TV for the market of Manipur requires different proportion. This proportion is determined from the number of pieces purchase - size-wise by the consumers of Manipur in the year 2001 (Table 38). The proportion of the sizes to be made available in Manipur is presented below.

Table 104
Size-wise proportion o/TV to be marketed in Manipur

Sizes in inch	*Proportion*
14	0.266
17	0.0063
20	0.172
21	0.373
25	0.046
29	0.0332
34	0.0025
Total	1.000

As a matter of fact, 81 % of the entire TV sales in Manipur come from 21 inches, 14 inches and 20 inches.

Product quality (attributes)

The main benefits or the attributes which the consumers of Manipur look for are picture quality, sound quality, and durability of the product (Table 70). These attributes are technical aspects of the product which the company should look into. Moreover, these things should be highlighted in advertisement or sales promotional activities of the marketer.

Warranty

Warranty is one of the marketing factors which produce

positive response of the consumers of Manipur in respect of buying TV (Table 72). Marketer can promote the product in Manipur by giving warranty because consumers infer that the TV is of high quality if it comes with warranty tag from the company.

Features

Foreign brands of TV with new technology are coming into the market. As a result, consumers have become more conscious about the various features of TV such as remote control, picture in picture, programming of channel, auto channel search, child lock, etc. And consumers are ready to pay more particularly for remote control, auto channel selection and child lock. As a matter of fact, consumers of Manipur are not going to buy those TV which do not have remote control facility. This aspect of the product decision should be considered while designing the product for Manipur market.

Price decision

Depending upon the affordability of the price of TV, consumers purchase TV at different price ranges. This should be taken into consideration while marketing TV in Manipur. The proportion of the TV sets to be marketed in Manipur is determined from the number of TV sets sold at different price ranges in Manipur in the year 2001. (Table 39).

Table 105
Price range and the proportion of TV sets of each price range to be marketed.

Price range	*Proportion*
Below Rs. 10,000/-	0.3772
Rs. 10,000/- but less than Rs. 15,000/-	0.3644
Rs. 15,000/- but less than Rs. 20,000/-	0.1419
Rs. 20,000/- but less than Rs. 25,000/-	0.102
Rs. 25,000/- and above	0.014
Total	1.000

To be precise, 74.16% of TV sales in Manipur in year 2001 are in the price below Rs.15,000/-. Easy instalment schemes is an effective marketing tool in respect of selling TV in Manipur (Table 80). If the company come out with an attractive easy instalment scheme particularly for the Govt. employees this will boost the sales of TV in Manipur.

Place decision

At present majority of TV buyers (69.65%) purchase TV sets from Imphal, the state capital of Manipur. About 24.04% purchase from nearby sub-dealers (Table 79).

Consumers of Manipur, when they purchase costly product, usually go to Imphal. But the problem they face is carrying of the product back home. If the main dealers in Imphal open sub-dealers in all the districts headquarters, this problem faced by consumers will be reasonably reduced. Consumers may come and see the products in the show room in Imphal and the delivery of the product can be made at district headquarters by the sub dealers. If this arrangement can be done, it will be an extra bonus to the buyers.

Promotion decision

In chapter 5, it is already discussed that the brand preference of TV is dependent on promotional strategies of the company and reference groups.

In the Table 84, it is revealed that in the purchase of a particular brand of TV, there is high involvement of other members of the family (Table 84). Main influencers are neighbours/relatives and co-workers/colleagues in the purchase of TV. (Table 75).

In the Table 74, 76 and 77, it is depicted that the main initiators are mother and youngsters, the main deciders are father and mother. And the main buyers are father and youngsters in the family.

In the Table 72, it is presented that the three marketing factors are product benefits, advertisement and warranty. Table 69 reveals that the main sources of information from which consumers comes to know about brand of TV are TV commercials, radio, newspaper and magazines.

With the help of the above information appropriate advertisement and sales promotional strategies can be designed as discuss below.

Advertising

Depending upon the financial position of the company, budget for advertisement can be decided by the marketer. For starting, marketer can spend what he can afford. Later, he can spend on the basis of the sales by taking certain percentage of sales proceeds as advertising budget.

Objectives of the advertisement should be to create the awareness of the brand as well as to educate consumers about the product (TV). Message of the advertisement should highlight the product benefits i.e., picture quality, sound quality and durability of the TV set. The illustration component of the advertisement copy (for print Ad) and the picturisation for advertisement in TV should centre around either family or social environment. This is due to the fact that the purchase decision of TV in Manipur involves other members of the family and the brand preference is dependent on their reference groups. The message should be desirable, exclusive and believable to the consumers of Manipur. Marketer should use emotional positioning approach (emotional appeal) as the TV buyers of Manipur are passive and emotional. (Chapter 5).

The message should be targeted to the initiators, deciders and buyers of a brand of TV.

Media vehicles

Depending upon the media habits of the consumers of

Manipur, following media are the appropriate vehicles for advertisement.

(Appendix V- media habits of consumers of Manipur).

Local newspaper (household)	*Share of readership (household)*	*Reach*
i) Sangai express	34.62%	35.77%
ii) Poknapham	34.36%	35.0%
Local magazine		
i) Athouba	25.31 %	5.31%
ii) Sanathong	46.83%	9.84%
National newspaper		
i) Telegraph	48.17%	26.32%
ii) Times of India	31.87%	17.42%
National magazine		
i) India Today	29.24%	13.96%.
ii) Outlook	14.20%	6.78%

For the TV Ad either in cable or Doordarshan, the appropriate timing for scheduling advertisement is in the evening when majority of the consumers watch TV programmes. To be precise, the timing of 6-9 p.m. (Appendix V Table J) is more appropriate for the consumers of Manipur because after 9 p.m., majority of the people go to sleep.

The effectiveness of the advertisement can be measured for (i) effectiveness of communication in terms of awareness through portfolio test (ii) effectiveness in terms of generating sales through sales effective research using experimental design of measuring sales before advertisement and after the advertisement.

Sales promotion

Purchase of TV is high during the marriage season in

Manipur. Giving a TV set by the parents of the bride as a gift in marriage is a custom in Manipur. About 23.38% of TV owners in Manipur got their TV as a gift in marriage. (Table 81).

Marriage season in Manipur spans over a period of 6 months from October to March. Average sales of TV during this period are higher by 30% to 40% than that of other months. People of Manipur have a positive response to the promotional strategies such as discount, free gift offers etc. leading to the purchase of TV. Apart from giving discount and free gift offers, if the company come out with attractive easy instalment scheme, chances are high for the company to capture the entire market. It can be mentioned here that 21.72% of the TV owners in Manipur purchased their TV through easy instalment scheme offer by the Manitron organisation and few dealers of other companies. (Table 80).

Marketer should also plan to promote their product in Manipur whenever there are major National/International sporting events. This is due to the fact that 25.53% of TV owners in Manipur purchased their TV during such sporting events. Games and sports culture prevailing in Manipur influences to a great extent the people to buy TV during such major sporting events. In essence, consumer oriented approach to marketing demands for managers who can feel the right pulse of their consumers. Mysteries of the consumer behaviour of Manipur in the purchase decisions of consumer non-durable goods and durable goods can be further unfolded through various motivational researches.

Appendix-I

Estimation of Purchase of Toilet Soap in India for the Year 2002

Table A
Worksheet for the analysis of time series by using least square method (for toilet soap volume)

Year	*Volume '000' tonnes y*	*X*	X^2	*XY*
1985-86	227.00	-4	16	- 908.00
1986-87	241.00	-3	9	- 723.00
1987-88	289.00	-2	4	- 578.00
1989-90	327.00	0	0	0.00
1992-93	433.51	+3	9	1300.53
1993-94	485.44	+4	16	1941.76
	$\Sigma Y = 2002.95$	$\Sigma x = -2$	$\Sigma X^2 = 54$	$\Sigma XY = 1033.29$

Let $Y = a + bx$ (i)

be the equation of the straight line trend. The two normal equations for solving the value of a and b are.

$\Sigma Y = aN + b\Sigma X$ (ii) where N is the number of observation

$\Sigma XY = a\Sigma x + b\Sigma X^2$ (iii)

by substituting the values in equation (ii) and (iii) we have,

$2002.95 = a.6 + b. (-2)$ (iv)

$1033.29 = a. (- 2) + b. 54$ (v)

by multiplying equation (v) by 3 and adding to equation (iv) we have,

$2002.95 + 3099.87 = - 2b + 162 b$

:. $b = 5103.82/160 = 31.89$

From equation no. (iv),

$a = (2002.95 + 2b)/ 6$

$= (2002.95 + 2x31.89)/ 6 = 2066.73/6$

$= 344.45$

Thus, the equation of the trend line given in equation (i) becomes $y = 344.45 + 31.89 X$

:. The projected sales of toilet soap in India up to the year 2001 are determined as given below by using the above equation.

For the Year	*(000) tones*
1993, put x = 4	Then y = 472.01
1994, put x = 5	Then y = 503.9
1995, put x = 6	Then y = 535.79
1996, put x = 7	Then y = 567.68
1997, put x = 8	Then y = 599.57
1998, put x = 9	Then y = 631.46
1999, put x = 10	Then y = 663.35
2000, put x = 11	Then y = 695.24
2001, put x = 12	Then y = 727.13

Appendix-II

Estimation of Domestic Consumption Value of Toilet Soap in India for the Year 2001

Table B
Worksheet for the analysis of time series by using least square method (for value of toilet soap)

Year	*Value in crore Y*	*X*	X^2	*XY*
1992-93	3985.5	- 2	4	- 7971.00
1993-94	4355.1	- 1	1	- 4355.1
1994-95	4644.3	0	0	0.00
1995-96	6248.3	1	1	6248.3
1996-97	6758.7	2	4	13517.4
1997-98	7477.4	3	9	22432.2
	$\Sigma y = 33469.3$	$\Sigma x = 3$	$\Sigma x^2 = 19$	$\Sigma xy = 29871.8$

Let $Y = a + bx$ (i)

be the equation of the straight line trend. The two normal equations for solving the value of a and b are.

$\Sigma Y = aN + b\Sigma X$ (ii) where N is the number of observation

$\Sigma XY = a\Sigma x + b\Sigma X^2$ (iii) by substituting the values in equation (ii) and (iii) we have,

33469.3 = a.6 + b.3 (iv)

29871.8 = a. 3 + b.19 (v)

by multiplying equation (v) by 2 and subtracting equation (iv) we have,

(59743.6 - 33469.3) = 38b - 3b

:. b = 26274.3/ 35 = 750.69

From equation no. (iv), we have

a = (33469.3-3b)/6

= (33469.3 - 3x750.69) 1 6 = 31217.23/6

= 5202.87

Then the equation of the trend line given in equation (i) becomes

y = 5202.87 + 750.69 X

:. The projected domestic consumption value of toilet soap in India up to the year

2001 are determined as given below by using the above equation.

For the year	*Value in crores*
1997, put x = 3	Then y = 7454.94
1998, put x = 4	Then y = 8205.63
1999, put x = 5	Then y = 8956.32
2000, put x = 6	Then y = 9707.01
2001, put x = 7	Then y = 10457.7

Appendix-III

Estimation of Purchase of TV Sets in India for the Year 2001

Table C
Worksheet for the analysis of time series by using least square method (for TV sets in units)

Year	*Units "million"*	*X*	*X^2*	*XY*
1985-86	2.00	-4	16	-8.00
1996-87	2.8	-3	9	-8.4
1987-88	3.6	-2	4	-7.2
1989-90	5.2	0	0	0.00
1992-93	4.22	3	9	12.66
1993-94	5.18	4	16	20.72
	$\Sigma y = 23.00$	$\Sigma x = -2$	$\Sigma x^2 = 54$	$\Sigma xy = 9.78$

Let Y = a+bx (i)

be the equation of the straight line trend. The two normal equations for solving the value of a and b are.

$\Sigma Y = aN + b\Sigma X$ (ii) where N is the number of observation

$\Sigma XY = a\Sigma x + b\Sigma X2$ (iii)

by substituting the values in equation (ii) and (iii) we have,

$23 = 6a - 2b$ (iv)

$9.78 = -2a + 54b$ (v)

by multiplying equation (v) by 3 and adding to equation (iv) we have,

$$29.34 + 23 = 162b - 2b$$

$$\therefore b = 52.34 / 160 = 0.327$$

from equation no. (iv), we have $a = (23 + 2b)/ 6$

$$= (23 + 2x0.327)/ 6 = 23.654/6$$

$$= 3.942$$

Then the equation of the trend line given in equation (i) becomes

$$y = 3.942 + 0.327 X$$

:. the projected purchase of TV in the Indian domestic market up to the year 2001 are determined as given below by using the above equation.

For the year	*Units in million*
1993, put x = 4	Then y = 5.25
1994, put x = 5	Then y = 5.577
1995, put x = 6	Then y = 5.904
1996, put x = 7	Then y = 6.231
1997, put x = 8	Then y = 6.558
1998, put x = 9	Then y = 6.885
1999, put x = 10	Then y = 7.212
2000, put x = 11	Then y = 7.539
2001, put x = 12	Then y = 7.866

Appendix-IV

Estimation of Domestic Consumption Value of TV in India for the Year 2001

Table D
Worksheet for the analysis of time series by using least square method (for TV sets by value)

Year	*Value in crore'y'*	*X*	*X^2*	*XY*
1992-93	2446.4	-2	4	-4892.8
1993-94	2946.6	-1	1	-2946.6
1994-95	2778.9	0	0	0.00
1995-96	3463.1	1	1	3463.1
1996-97	4204.3	2	4	8408.6
1997-98	5478.00	3	9	16434.00
	$\Sigma y = 21317.3$	$\Sigma x = 3$	$\Sigma x^2 = 19$	$\Sigma xy = 20466.3$

Let Y = a+bx (i)

be the equation of the straight line trend. The two normal equations for solving the value of a and b are.

$\Sigma Y = aN + b\Sigma X$ (ii) where N is the number of observation

$\Sigma XY = a\Sigma x + b\Sigma X2$ (iii)

by substituting the values in equation (ii) and (iii) we have,

$21317.3 = 6a + 3b$ (iv)
$20466.3 = 3a + 19b$ (v)

by multiplying equation (v) by 2 and substracting equation (iv) we have,

40932.6 - 21317.3 = 38b - 3b

:. b = 19615.3/35 = 5660.43

From equation no. (iv), we have a = (21317.3 – 3b)/6

= 19636.01/6 = 3272.66

Then the equation of the trend line given in equation (i) becomes

y = 3272.66 + 560.43 X

:. the projected purchase of TV in the Indian domestic market up to the year 2001 are determined as given below by using the above equation.

For the year	*Value in crores*
1997, put x = 3	Then y = 4953.95
1998, put x = 4	Then y = 5514.38
1999, put x = 5	Then y = 6074.81
2000, put x = 6	Then y = 6635.24
2001, put x = 7	Then y = 7195.67

Appendix-V

Present Media Habits of the Consumers of Manipur 2002

Table E

Subscriber/non subscriber of local newspapers, local magazines, national newspapers and national magazines

Newspaper/ Magazine	*No of Households – District-wise*					
	Bishnupur	*Thoubal*	*Imphal East*	*Imphal West*	*Churchand-pur*	*Total*
Local newspaper						
Subscriber	154	139	129	158	92	672
Non subscriber	19	12	22	21	6	80
Total	173	151	151	179	98	752
% of subscriber	89.01	92.05	85.43	88.26	93.87	89.36
Local magazine						
Subscriber	45	39	29	22	69	204
Non subscriber	128	112	122	157	29	548
Total	173	151	151	179	98	752
% of subscriber	26.01	25.82	19.20	12.29	70.40	27.12
National newspaper						
Subscriber	64	57	70	109	60	360
Non subscriber	109	94	81	70	38	392
Total	173	151	151	179	98	752
% of subscriber	36.99	60.63	46.35	60.89	61.22	47.87
National magazine						
Subscriber	43	56	48	92	54	293
Non subscriber	130	95	103	87	44	459
Total	173	151	151	179	98	752
% of subscriber	24.85	37.08	28.47	51.39	55.10	38.96

Table F
Local newspaper; share of readership (by households) and reach (by households)

Newspaper/ Magazine	*No of Households – District-wise*							
	Bishnupur	*Thoubal*	*Imphal East*	*Imphal West*	*Churchandpur*	*Total*	*% Share of Readership*	*% of Reach*
1. Sangai	67	56	41	72	33	269	34.62	35.77
2. Yakairol	9	13	7	3		32	4.11	4.25
3. Poknaham	66	56	62	81	2	267	34.36	35.50
4. Free Press	4	1	21	33	8	67	8.62	8.90
5. Thoudang	21	5	14			40	5.14	5.31
6. Huiyen Lanpao	4	10	13	24		51	6.56	6.76
7. Other			14	11	26	51	6.56	6.76
Total						777	100	—

Note 1 Some households subscribe more than one local newspaper.
Note 2 reach is calculated from the total sample households of 752.

Table G
Local magazine; share of readership (by households) and reach (by households)

Newspaper/ Magazine	*No of Households – District-wise*							
	Bishnupur	*Thoubal*	*Imphal East*	*Imphal West*	*Churchandpur*	*Total*	*% Share of Readership*	*% of Reach*
1. Athouba	13	16	4	7		40	25.91	5.31
2. Sanathong	26	16	13	19		74	46.83	9.84
3. Anouba Mangol		12				12	7.59	1.59
4. Echema		3				3	1.89	0.39
5. Panthung			4			4	2.53	0.53
6. Macha Leima			9			9	5.69	1.19
7. Eikhoigee Yaol			4			4	2.53	0.53
8. Others	1	1			10	12	7.59	1.59
Total						158	100	—

Table H
National newspaper; share of readership (by households) and reach (by households)

Newspaper/ Magazine	*No of Households – District-wise*							
	Bishnupur	*Thoubal*	*Imphal East*	*Imphal West*	*Churchandpur*	*Total*	*% Share of Readership*	*% of Reach*
1. Telegraph	34	27	44	66	27	198	48.17	26.32
2. Times of India	20	23	25	39	24	131	31.87	17.42
3. Asian Age	2	4	7	7	3	23	5.59	3.05
4. Hindustan Times	2	4	5	2	4	17	4.13	2.26
5. Others	2		10	25	5	42	10.21	5.58
Total						411	100	—

Table I
National magazine; share of readership (by households) and reach (by households)

Newspaper/ Magazine	*No of Households – District-wise*							
	Bishnupur	*Thoubal*	*Imphal East*	*Imphal West*	*Churchandpur*	*Total*	*% Share of Readership*	*% of Reach*
1. Outlook	5	4	13	22	7	51	14.20	6.78
2. Competition Success Review	4	8	4	2	13	31	8.62	4.12
3. India Today	10	17	19	42	17	105	29.24	13.96
4. Femina	5	3	7	14	3	32	8.91	4.25
5. Frontline	2	6	2	5	14	29	8.07	3.85
6. Reader Digest	11	2	4	14	3	34	9.47	4.52
7. Sports Star	4	3	5		5	17	4.73	2.26
8. Sunday	2	3	5	5	2	17	4.73	2.26
9. Others	8	12	14	5	4	43	11.97	5.71
Total						359	100	—

Table J
Timing of watching TV; share of different timings

Timing	*No. of Persons – District-wise*					*Total*	*% Share of Readership*
	Bishnupur	*Thoubal*	*Imphal East*	*Imphal West*	*Churchandpur*		
6-9 am	17	29	21	12	22	101	12.25
9 am.-12 noon	35	4	16	17	17	89	10.80
12 noon - 3 pm.	11	10	15	18	22	76	9.22
3 – 6 pm.	17	21	21	30	36	125	15.16
6- 9 pm	30	67	40	66	43	246	29.85
9 - 12 midnight	6	18	46	63	42	175	21.23
After midnight	2	1	2	3	4	12	1.45
Total						824	100

Note: some individuals indicate more than one of the timings indicated in the response category of watching TV.

Appendix-VI

Profile of the 752 Sampled Respondents

Table K
Age Profile

Age	No. of Respondents – District-wise					Total	%
	Bishnupur	Thoubal	Imphal East	Imphal West	Churchandpur		
Below 21	18	13	15	5	24	75	9.97
21–30	63	63	50	74	45	295	39.22
31–40	40	48	41	65	17	211	28.05
41–50	31	19	29	15	11	105	13.96
51–60	16	7	12	12	1	48	6.38
Total	173	151	151	179	98	752	100

Table L
Religion Profile

Religion	No. of Respondents – District-wise					Total	%
	Bishnupur	Thoubal	Imphal East	Imphal West	Churchandpur		
Hindu	157	139	130	144	2	572	76.06
Muslim	2	5	1	2		10	1.32
Christian	8		3	13	95	119	15.82
Meitei	5	7	17	17		46	6.11
Sikh				1		1	0.13
Jain				2		2	0.26
Buddhist					1	1	0.13
Vaisnabi	1					1	0.13
Total	173	151	151	179	98	752	100

Table M
Educational qualification

Educational Qualification	*No. of Respondents – District-wise* Bishnupur	Thoubal	Imphal East	Imphal West	Church-andpur	Total	%
Below X	5	1	5	11		22	2.92
X	34	29	30	12	24	129	17.15
X+2	34	40	35	27	15	151	20.07
Graduate	79	60	67	81	45	332	44.14
Post Graduate	17	20	10	37	14	98	13.03
Doctor			2	3		5	0.66
Engineer	4	1	2	8		15	1.99
Total	173	151	151	179	98	752	100

Table N
Profile of family characteristics of the respondents

Religion	*No. of Respondents – District-wise* Bishnupur	Thoubal	Imphal East	Imphal West	Church-andpur	Total	%
a	50	64	39	54	32	239	31.78
b	15	16	13	19	11	74	9.84
c	32	29	24	25	24	134	17.81
d	28	13	12	14	11	78	10.37
e	44	29	56	56	18	203	26.99
f	1		2	6		9	1.19
g	1		2	2		5	0.66
h	2		2	3	2	9	1.19
i			1			1	0.13
Total	173	151	151	179	98	752	100

Where

a. Single
b. Newly married couple with no children

c. Young married couple with youngest child under six years.
d. Young married couple with youngest child above six years.
e. Older married couple with dependent children
f. Older married couple with no children living with them & head of the household is still working.
g. Older married couple with no children living at home & head of the family is retired. h. Lone survivor in the family, still working
i. Lone survivor, retired.

Table 0
Occupation profile

	No. of Households – District-wise						
Occupation	*Bishnupur*	*Thoubal*	*Imphal East*	*Imphal West*	*Church-andpur*	*Total*	*%*
a	14	35	4	10	2	65	8.64
b	6	14	16	9	10	55	7.31
c	39	29	59	50	26	203	26.99
d	21	7	10	28	21	87	11.56
e	10	4	9	5	2	30	3.99
F	15	14	11	8	2	50	6.64
g	22	22	20	44	13	121	16.09
h	16	5	4	11	3	39	5.18
i	30	21	18	19	19	102	13.56
Total	173	151	151	179	98	752	100

Where

a. Farmer
b. Wage earner / laborer
c. Govt. employee
d. Qualified Professional (Technical qualified, self employed).
e. Artisans (Skilled workers like blacksmith, carpenter, mason who work independently and not on salary come under this category)

f. Shopkeeper (owner's of retail shop i.e.tea stall, pan dukan, grocery shop etc.)

g. Businessman (other than shopkeepers)

h. Housewife (who is not earning but who takes household decisions)

i. Any other includes students and unemployed.

Table P
Monthly family income profile

	No. of Respondents– District-wise						
Income	*Bishnupur*	*Thoubal*	*Imphal East*	*Imphal West*	*Church-andpur*	*Total*	*%*
a	34	45	22	30	22	163	21.67
b	99	75	80	49	25	328	43.61
c	24	15	22	29	12	102	13.56
d	9	13	10	30	16	78	10.37
e	4	3	4	16	7	34	4.52
f	1		3	5	4	13	1.72
g				6	4	10	1.32
h	2			7	4	13	1.72
i				7	4	11	1.46
Total	151		151	179	98	752	100

Where

(a) Below Rs 5000 (b) 500 I – 10000

(c) 10001- 15000 (d) 15001- 20000

(e) 20001- 25000 (f) 25001- 30000

(g) 30001- 40000 (h) 40001 and above

Occupation and income profile of the respondents who do not presently own TV

Table Q
Occupation profile

Occupation	No. of Respondents– District-wise					Total	% Share of Readership
	Bishnupur	Thoubal	Imphal East	Imphal West	Churchandpur		
a	4	12	3	9	2	30	20.13
b		4	12	7	9	32	21.47
c		5	4	5	11	25	16.77
d		1		2	8	11	7.38
e	2	1	2		1	6	4.02
f	1	2	5		2	10	6.71
g	2		2	3	5	12	8.05
h		1	2	3	1	7	4.69
i	2	6			8	16	10.73
Total	11	32	30	31	45	149	100

Where,

a. Farmer

b. Wager earner / laborer

c. Govt. employee

d. Qualified Professional (Technical qualified, self-employed).

e. Artisans (Skilled workers like blacksmith, carpenter, mason who work independently and not on salary come under this category)

f. Shopkeeper (owner's of retail shop i.e., tea stall, pan dukan, grocery shop etc.)

g. Businessman (other than shopkeepers)

h. Housewife (who is not earning but who takes household decisions

i. Any other include students and unemployed

Table R
Monthly income of the households which do not presently own TV till March 2001

Religion	*No. of Respondents– District-wise*					*Total*	*% Share of Reader-ship*
	Bishnupur	*Thoubal*	*Imphal East*	*Imphal West*	*Church-andpur*		
a	10	20	24	25	19	98	65.77
b	1	11	5	5	12	34	22.81
c		1	1	1	2	5	3.35
d					4	4	2.68
e					2	2	1.34
f					3	3	2.01
g					2	2	1.34
h					1	1	0.67
Total	11	32	30	31	45	149	100

Note: Some part of the Churahndpur district could not be reached by TV signal Because of this reason some of the households inspite of having high family.

(a) Below Rs 5000 (b) 5001 – 1000

(c) 10001- 15000 (d) 15001- 20000

(e) 20001- 25000 (f) 25001- 30000

(g) 3000 1- 40000 (h) 40001 and above

Bibliography

Agarwal A N (1996), *Indian Economy*, 22nd Edition, Wishwa Prakashan, New Delhi.

Chunawala S A and Sethia K C (1997), *Foundation of Advertising - Theory and Practice,* 4th Edition, Himalaya Publishing House, New Delhi.

David Luke J and Donald Robin S (1997), *Marketing Research,* 7th edition, Prentice Hall of India, New Delhi.

Donald Tull S and Del Hawkins I (1996), *Marketing Research—Measurement and Methods,* 6th Edition, Prentice Hall of India, New Delhi.

Gupta S P (1995), *Statistical Method*, Revised Edition, Sultan Chand and Sons Publishers, New Delhi.

Hans Raj (1996), *Theory and Practices in Social Research,* 5th Edition, Surjeet Publications,New Delhi.

Harper W Boyd, Jr. Ralph West Fell and Stanley F Stasch (1994), *Marketing Research*, 7th Edition, All India Traveller Book Sellers, New Delhi.

Henry Assael (1998), *Consumer Behaviour*, 6th Edition, Asian Books Pvt. Ltd., NewDelhi.

James Stonner A F and Freeman Edward(1992), *Management*, 5th Edition, Prentice Hall of India, New Delhi.

Khan Martin (2001), *Consumer Behaviour*, New Age International Publisher, New Delhi.

Kothari C R (1996), *Research Methodology - Methods and Techniques*, 2nd Edition, Wishwa Prakashan, New Delhi.

Leon Schiffman G and Leslie Lazar Kanuk(1997), *Consumer Behaviour*, 6th Edition, Prentice Hall of India, New Delhi.

Manorama Year Book 2001, Malayala Manorama, New Delhi.

Mehta P L (1993), *Managerial Economics*, 6th edition, Sultan Chand & Sons Publication, New Delhi.

Michael V P(1996), *Research Methodology in Management*, 3rd Edition, Himayala Publishing House, New Delhi

N.N. Sachitanand (1999), "Consumer Durable - Indian brands dominate and fast moving consumer goods - MNCs strengthen grip," *Survey of Indian Industries*, Hindu Publication, New Delhi.

Philip Kotler (1999), *Marketing Management*, 10th Edition, Prentice Hall of India, New Delhi.

Philip Kotler and Armstrong Gary (2001), *Principles of Marketing*, 9th Edition, Prentice Hall of India, New Delhi.

Philip Kotler and Gary Armstrong, *Principles of Marketing*, 7th Edition, Prentice Hall of India, Eastern Economy Edition, New Delhi.

Philip Kotler (1991), *Principles of Marketing*, 7th Edition, Prentice Hall of India, New Delhi.

Ramanuj Majumdar (2000), *Product Management in India*, 2nd Edition, Prentice Hall of India, New Delhi.

Rao K V (1995), *Research Methodology in Management*, Sterling Publisher Pvt. Ltd., New Delhi.

Rao S L and Natarajan I(1996), *Indian Demographic*, Global Business Press, New Delhi.

Richard Leven I. and David Rubin S (1997), *Statistics for Management*, Prentice Hall of India, New Delhi.

Rathor B.S (1990), *Advertising Management*, Himayala Publishing House, First Edition, New Delhi.

"*Statistical Abstracts of Manipur - 2001*", Directorate of Economics & Statistics, Govt. of Manipur, Imphal.

Index

■■■